Twelve Dead Men Speak

Twelve Dead Men Speak

David Shearman

Sovereign World

Sovereign World Ltd
PO Box 777
Tonbridge
Kent TN11 0ZS
England

ISBN 1 85240 340 3

Cover design by CCD, www.ccdgroup.co.uk
Typeset by CRB Associates, Reepham, Norfolk
Printed by Clays Ltd, St. Ives plc

Contents

Foreword

This is a timely book both for prophetic people and for leaders. Potential prophets will gain an understanding of context and focus. Context determines what God wants to say. Focus is required when processing your own identity and calling with regard to the nation you inhabit. In studying the lives of these twelve brave, dedicated men, we can determine the identity, courage and sacrifice required to speak to a nation.

Leaders should read this book to further understand the type of church that must be built in these days. The nation badly needs to see a company of people living in the favour of God and prophetically speaking out into an increasingly chaotic and unjust society.

I appreciate David's fearlessness, candour and integrity. I have seen at first hand his love for both his country and the wider body of Christ. His commitment to excellence as a leader and a father figure is the only way to truly honour and represent the Lord.

This is an excellent thought-provoking book – I hope leaders and prophetic people care enough about their country to want to be adjusted by the truth.

Graham Cooke
March 2003

Acknowledgements

To my wife, family and friends who make my life a garden of beauty.

To Howard Satterthwaite, my young lawyer friend, now in Kenya, for his unstinting commitment to the project during his six month internship.

To Malcolm Baxter and Jamie Fyleman for their support during the latter stages of writing and to Andy Green for the application, yet again, of his considerable linguistic and grammar skills – all making a better book.

To Sarah Smellie, who returned as a mother, and put huge energy into the gathering and production of the final manuscript.

And above all, to the Abba of Jesus – Thank you.

Introduction

Winston Churchill said, "The farther backward you look, the farther forward you are likely to see." The twelve Minor Prophets of the Bible prophesied into the life and times of nations more than 2500 years ago. Reading them is to look backward a long way. Understanding what they teach is to see farther forward than would otherwise be likely. Our generation with its post-modern message and neo-pagan ways would be wise to attend to their words.

There is an overriding spiritual, social and moral summary to the message of the twelve dead men. It can be stated simply and starkly. God will eventually hold any individual, community or nation responsible for ignoring and forgetting Him. This provides both a personal and a corporate challenge.

There are two overriding conclusions that can be drawn from this statement. Firstly, many of the problems in our society are directly or indirectly attributable to our forgetting God and worshipping other things. This provides a philosophical challenge. Secondly, no amount of money, ingenuity and effort will alone solve these problems. The solution must include the addressing of our spiritual needs and returning to God as a priority. This provides a practical challenge.

As we shall be looking at each prophet's message in the order they appear in the Bible, it will help you to have a Bible available as you read. My words, although seeking to deliver a contemporary relevance, are not to be compared with the inspired Word of God.

I pray that you will understand that these men who spoke God's truth in ancient times are still speaking, with sometimes frightening clarity, to the Now generation.

HOSEA
(c. 770–730 BC)

❧ ☙

Chapter 1

Hedonism Unmasked

"All that glisters is not gold."
(Shakespeare)

It was a time of peace and plenty. The great neighbouring empires of Assyria and Egypt, due to poor leadership and natural disasters, were in decline. The yoke around Israel's neck had been loosed, and Israel was swift to take full advantage of the favourable position in which she now found herself. Exercising her growing prosperity and power, she marched with rapid strides into the surrounding nations, extending her geographical boundaries and cultural influences. Wealth once again poured into the nation of Israel as she reclaimed governance of the main trading routes – governance she cashed in on with a carefree policy of commercial and economic development.[1]

Israel's economy was booming. Her cities thrived in a frenzied climate of expansion and urbanisation. The wealthy wallowed in their new-found affluence with an impudent display of indifference, and a new middle class emerged to enjoy unprecedented wealth – eager to indulge themselves in all that their money could buy. The pursuit of pleasure (most notably drunkenness and sexual promiscuity) was high on most people's agenda. The seeds of prosperity, power and multiculturalism had given birth to a new Israel – a heavyweight hedonistic society, punch drunk with pleasure.

But God was angry. He saw through the smokescreen of transient pleasure to the pain and misery that lay beneath. From

11

the depths of His unfailing love and concern for His people, and His ancient and oft-repeated promises, He saw idolatry, He saw vile practices, including the sacrifice of children. He saw materialism with an indifference to the growing inequality in wealth and opportunity. He saw how bitterly the people of Israel were suffering.

The people saw a fruit that looked good on the outside, but Hosea showed them the rotten core. The people were content with their futile pleasures; the prophet reminded them of their forgotten promises. The people thought that things had never been so good and were set to continue; the prophet told them that God was about to transform their situation, bringing judgement and calamity. Time and time again the words of the prophet chastise, but they also comfort, constantly reassuring the people of God's love and desire to bless them without overlooking their gross and unfaithful behaviour.

The book of Hosea can be broken down into four simple sections:

- Chapters 1 to 3 outline the story of Hosea's life and marriage, using them as a parable. Hosea's love and accept-ance of a wayward wife is a reflection of God's love and desire for His disobedient people.

- Chapters 4 to 7 detail the general and specific indictments of the sins of Israel, with a special call to repentance in chapter 6:1–3.

- Chapters 8 to 10 provide a warning of the impending judgement and punishment that the unrepentant nation would receive. They specify the Assyrian nation as the group God would use to fulfil Hosea's predictions.

- Chapters 11 to 14 repeat the truth of the opening parable, expressing God's incessant love, the nation's sin, and the assurance that genuine repentance and change of attitude and lifestyle would bring God's blessing to them once again.

Hosea's words concentrate around three themes: sin, judgement and love. Let us hear more of them and see what they contain appropriate and relevant to our lives and our nations.

Sin

Imagine a high court. The words, "What are the charges?" ring out. The defendants rise to stand as a lawyer, the prophet Hosea, reads out the prosecution charges: *"There is no faithfulness, no love, no acknowledgement of God in the land. There is only cursing, lying and murder, stealing and adultery; they break all bounds and bloodshed follows bloodshed. Because of this the land mourns"* (4:1–3).

The first of the accused to be collectively singled out by Hosea are Israel's religious leaders. *"My people are destroyed from lack of knowledge. Because you have rejected knowledge, I also reject you as my priests; because you have ignored the law of God, I also will ignore your children"* (4:6). After further strong words of censure, the remaining defendants are addressed. *"Pay attention you Israelites! Listen, O royal house! This judgement is against you"* (5:1). He speaks of arrogance, rebellion, prostitution, corruption, and that *"They are unfaithful to the LORD"* (5:7).

Like the people that Hosea spoke to, we know that our society is not as it should be. Hosea did not spend much time describing society's social ills. He simply told the people that the way they were living was sinful and displeasing to God, and would lead to dire consequences unless they changed their ways. That said, some rigour on my part is required to amplify the present state of our nations.

The chattering classes point to a community of tolerance, more choices, economic improvement for the majority, longer living and better health care. The list is like a self-convincing mantra. There are many facts and statistics, both positive and negative, that fuel the argument concerning the present condition of our countries. Beyond these facts and statistics, what are the deeper issues? The importance of our spirituality and our spiritual needs is a huge and often neglected – but relevant – requirement for a rich and righteous society. In answer to the question, "Why do your writings have little visible spiritual content?" Warren Bennis (adviser to four US Presidents and author of many books) recently commented that academia had been secularised. Could it be that the forces of secularisation in our nations have contributed to the present condition of the world in which we live?

The Judeo-Christian heritage of Western civilisation provided a legal, moral and spiritual foundation for civil society. This heritage has profoundly benefited our lives and our communities: from education and health care to the value of the individual, the sanctity of marriage and commitment to the family; from the structure of law to the way we trade. All this and much more was directly influenced from a profoundly spiritual and biblical base. Generations of Christians sacrificed much, devoting large parts of their lives to the development of a just society.

To substantiate this claim, let me introduce you to some Christians. William Wilberforce in the late eighteenth century played a pivotal role in the abolition of slavery. Dr Kate Bushnell was a fundamental figure in the creation of laws abolishing forced prostitution in the US. The Earl of Shaftsbury, Anthony Cooper, pioneered the abolition of child labour in the UK. His counterpart Edgar Murphy was the prime mover behind the abolition of child labour in the US. Brave and courageous Christians, perhaps none more so than Martin Luther King, have daringly fought for racial equality in countries throughout the world. And William Booth founded the Salvation Army, the UK's largest independent welfare provider today. These are some of the public figures among an army of millions who have affected our society for good.

There is something wrong with the Western world. It stands proud with its head held high – a well-ordered, caring, imaginative and prosperous society – but it is a fool's paradise. It has become a world which fails to recognise the catastrophic danger of neglecting the precious spiritual foundation which so greatly influenced its development. Brick by brick it has allowed the foundations to be torn away leaving it in danger of collapse. In the words of the Chief Rabbi, Dr Jonathan Sacks,

> "We made a simple, well-intentioned assumption. But a wrong one. Namely, that there are only two institutions that can deal with social problems, either the state or the market ... [We] have focused on institutions which reinforce behaviour rather than change it: government which reflects votes, politics which follow opinion polls, therapies that tell us that we are OK as we are, markets that mirror our choices. Where in culture will we find something that gives us the power to change? In these covenantal institutions of families and communities ... I believe the time has now come for our faith communities to become a counter-cultural presence, a force to challenge the tin gods of fame and power and success which are great for those who win, but hell for those who lose; and to protest against a world, a society, that knows the price of everything and the value of nothing, as it travels the road of economic affluence and spiritual poverty, of ever stronger governments and markets and ever weaker families and communities."[2]

"But," many Western citizens will argue, "just wait a minute. We're prosperous – many of us have never had it so good. Who is God, and who needs him anyway? We're doing okay on our own, thank you very much!" It is time to take off our rose-tinted spectacles and face up to the severity of the social, moral and spiritual decay in our apparently healthy society.

1.3 billion people (21% of the world's population) have to live on less than 70p (110 US cents) per day.[3]

In the US a human being over the age of 12 is sexually assaulted **every two minutes**.[4]

Read your newspapers: teenage boys head-butt police officers and attack teachers. Our future generation abuse, steal and murder – sadly, they are predominantly the result of our own generation's depravity. Hundreds of thousands of fathers have lost contact with their sons and daughters. Babies are used as human ashtrays. Paedophiles prey on young children. Husbands batter their wives and some wives batter their husbands.

As a Christian leader, I must take seriously the prophet's observations about the priesthood. They were singled out ahead of the nation, the people and the royal family for condemnation and judgement. Why? Because they had ignored the law of their God (4:6). Their poor leadership was part of the nation's problems. They compromised the truth, they were silent about the people's idolatry and colluded with their turning away from God. God blamed them for contributing to the general state of immorality in the nation. He was obliged to act.

There have been too many examples of collusion, compromise and silence by Christian leaders in our societies. In August 2002, for example, a highly-publicised survey conducted by Christian Research revealed that a third of Church of England clergy – a prominent part of Britain's "priesthood" – doubt or disbelieve in the physical resurrection of Jesus Christ. Only half are convinced of the truth of the virgin birth. The poll of nearly two thousand of the Church's ten thousand clergy also found that only half believe that faith in Christ is the only route to salvation.[5]

Those who are involved in Christian leadership must not bow to the forces of secular society. They must hold true to the Bible. They must not water-down the truth or whitewash the sins of their nations.

Like the Israelites, the second group of defendants, many of us are guilty of failing to acknowledge God. Sadly, even in parts of society where prayers are said and God's name is spoken, these practices are often merely "religious", being unaccompanied by godly thoughts or actions.

The religious leaders and the Israelites (you and me) are not alone in the dock: the royal house, the third group of defendants are keeping them (and us) company. In our analogy, the "royal house" is not limited in its scope to royal families as we know them today. People with power, authority and influence – presidents, prime ministers, senators and members of parliament come within this category. Are the people in these positions of responsibility, men and women elected by the people, making the right decisions and forming the right policies? Or have they ignored the spiritual dimension, the fundamental ingredient in the recipe for a fully functional, fulfilled, just and righteous society?

So what can be said of sin? My experiences have taught me this truth: sin always costs more than you want to pay, takes you further than you want to go and keeps you longer than you want to stay. To quote Campbell Morgan, "Sin, in its last analysis, in its most horrible form, is infidelity to love. It hurts God, it destroys the sinner. God can never condone sin, but He can and does redeem the sinner. "

Judgement

> "Everybody wants to see justice done – to somebody else."
> *Bruce Cockburn*

In our modern age judgement – divine wrath or punishment – is unfashionable. It is generally ignored to maintain a more comfortable but incomplete picture of God. God, however, cannot be wholly holy without judgement. Judgement, love, compassion and the many other facets of God's character are all indispensable elements of His identity. We may rightly shudder at His great holiness, His great anger and condemnation of injustice – but we must not close our eyes to His judgement.

Hosea spoke out God's judgement, His commitment to take action against the Israelites for their sins: *"So I will destroy your mother ... I also will ignore your children ... And it will be: Like people, like priests. I will punish both of them for their ways and repay them for their deeds"* (4:5–6 and 9).

God promised that His judgement would arrive in two ways: progressively like a moth eating cloth (5:12); and suddenly like a great lion tearing its prey to pieces (5:14). *"Then"*, He says, *"I will go back to my place until they admit their guilt . . . in their misery they will earnestly seek me"* (5:15). The words continue statement after statement, several chapters of terrifying penalties are decreed in response to the Israelites rebellion and idolatry.

We have allowed the wool to be pulled over our eyes. As I write and you read, the moth is eating away at the fabric of our society. The downward spiral of Western civilisation away from God is a reality we must all face. The Bible explicitly defines this progressive descent into darkness in Romans 1:18–32, and invalidates ignorance as a defence to the prophets' charge.

By way of example, the UK looks set to derail the long-standing blasphemy law. The blasphemy law relates directly to the third Commandment given by God (Exodus 20:7), a historic cornerstone of our nation's laws, and is part of the very foundation of a fully-functioning, just and righteous society. If you take away this law, by definition you have made a decision – the God of our fathers, the pre-existing Almighty God, does not exist. Because if He does, we must obey Him.

In Hosea's day the majority of people ignored the warning. History records that what God said would happen, did happen: the nation of Israel was devastated by the Assyrians in 722 BC and would never again return to her former glory. Why should we think that an unchanging God will deal with our civilisation any differently? We have been warned. Preaching in London many years ago Billy Graham said, "If God does not judge Western society He will have to apologise to Sodom and Gomorrah."

Love

Like many of the prophets, Hosea spoke hard words and delivered searing judgements, but he also brought a message of love. Eugene Peterson expresses this side of Hosea's prophecy most eloquently:

"We live in a world awash in love stories. Most of them are lies. They are not love stories at all – they are lust stories, sex-fantasy stories, domination stories. From the cradle we are fed on lies about love. This would be bad enough if it only messed up human relationships – man and woman, parent and child, friend and friend – but it also messes up God-relationships. The huge, mountainous reality of all exist-ence is that God is love, that God loves the world. Each single detail of the real world that we face and deal with day after day is permeated by this love. But when our minds and imaginations are crippled with lies about love, we have a hard time understanding this fundamental ingredient of daily living, 'love', either as a noun or as a verb. And if the basic orienting phrase 'God is love' is plastered over with cultural graffiti that obscure and deface the truth of the way the world is, we are not going to get very far in living well. We require true stories of love if we are to live truly."[6]

Let's talk about love. What is it? The dictionary defines love as: "To feel great affection and sexual attraction for . . . to enjoy very much . . . to like very much."[7] Do we really know, feel or experience true love? Is love nothing more than great affection and sexual attraction? Society's menacing misrepresentation of love is everywhere; in magazines, newspapers, television and advertising; it's out there, just waiting for its next victim; seeking out its prey; it is an evil distortion of the truth – a lie.

We must not fall into the trap we've had set for ourselves. Sex is a joyous act made for marriage, a relationship designed for absolute trust and commitment. It must not be abused. Sex is not a recreational sport. Sex with anyone in any circumstance is not something to be desired. It is like a time bomb concealed in pretty pink paper – and the clock is ticking. Eventually it will explode, however long the fuse. Chasing after lovers, indulging in prostitutes, letching over pornographic pictures, or any other seedy sexual craving will not fill the emptiness in the core of mankind. This road leads only to the misery of a restless desire for more which will never be satisfied.

Love is so much more than we are led to believe.

> *"Love is patient, love is kind. It does not envy, it does not boast, it is not proud. It is not rude, it is not self-seeking, it is not easily angered, it keeps no record of wrongs. Love does not delight in evil but rejoices with the truth. It always protects, always trusts, always hopes, always perseveres. Love never fails."*
>
> (1 Corinthians 13:4–8).

Love is more devotion than emotion. It is not exclusively based on our emotions. Without doubt our emotions are involved but they must not be our only criterion for love. Our touchstone should be action – true devotion will always lead to action – true love.[8]

God reveals His awesome, limitless love for all humankind through Hosea's loving acceptance of his adulterous wife in the face of her unfaithful, disgusting and hurtful behaviour. Yet Hosea's reconciliation with his wife (3:1) stands as a mere echo of the magnitude of God's deep-seated desire to reconcile His rebellious people – you and me – to Himself.

Thousands of years later, in our present age, the unfaithful spouse appears far too frequently in the tapestry of our society. Men and women are awash with the pain and anguish of betrayal. It is all too easy to imagine the heartache and the hurt that wells up inside those who have been betrayed: feelings of anger, disgust and rejection. Trust which has been destroyed may take longer than a lifetime to heal.

But, here's the punch line: God's love overcomes. Amidst heart-breaking emotions He doesn't turn His back. He doesn't divorce us and cut all ties. Instead, He courts us and makes advances to us. Burning with passion, He sings songs of love to us, desiring us to draw near to Him, to be in union with Him. We're the apple of His eye! He's infatuated with us, wretched, selfish sinners that we are! Make no mistake – He's not blinded by His love for us. He knows every awful detail of our rebellion. This is not holy lust or fantasised emotion, but an amazing act of devotion – genuine love with no strings attached. His passion for us is amazing:

"Therefore I am going to allure her; I will lead her into the desert and speak tenderly to her. There I will give her back her vineyards, and will make the Valley of Achor a door of hope. There she will sing as in the days of her youth, as in the day she came up out of Egypt. 'In that day,' declares the LORD, 'You will call me "my husband"; you will no longer call me "my master". I will remove the names of the Baals from her lips; no longer will their names be invoked. In that day I will make a covenant for them with the beasts of the fields and the birds of the air and the creatures that move along the ground. Bow and sword and battle I will abolish from the land, so that all may lie down in safety. I will betroth you to me forever; I will betroth you in righteousness and justice, in love and compassion. I will betroth you in faithfulness, and you will acknowledge the LORD.'" (2:14–20)

God calls us by names that not only express His displeasure but also reveal the truth of how we live: *Lo-Ruhamah* – "not loved" and *Lo-Ammi* – "not my people" (1:6 and 9). He places dynamite at the gates of the prison where we're held captive by lies about love. Where we're smothered by deception, believing that this is all we deserve, that this is all we're worth, God blasts the gates open as wide as His loving arms. Releasing us from our gaol, He tells us who we really are: *"Say of your brothers, 'My people', and of your sisters, 'My loved one'"* (2:1).

The seventeen-year-old Cassie Bernell wrote three days before she was gunned down in the Columbine School Massacre of her love for Jesus Christ. It exemplifies the passion of someone responding to God's love. "Now I have given up on everything else – I have found it to be the only way to really know Christ and to experience the mighty power that brought Him back to life again, and to find out what it means to suffer and to die with Him. So whatever it takes, I will be one who lives in the fresh newness of life of those who are alive from the dead" (Cassie Bernell – 18 April, 1999).[9]

We live in a world where people have much, share little and

are satisfied less. We live in a society driven by many forces to the next event, the next purchase, the next orgasm, but remain out of breath and unfulfilled. In this environment, it is all too easy to allow God's tender tones of love to be drowned out as He speaks to us, warning us that our present behaviour will be our ruin.

Our conduct must change: our idolatry, loving and worshipping other things in place of God. Our rebellion, including writing laws that disobey God's law. Our adultery, ignoring our covenantal promises. Our arrogance, thinking that we can run and control all things without recognising that God created everything, including us. All these attitudes and actions carry severe penalties.

What you sow, you will reap; how you live today will have a bearing on what happens tomorrow. In love, through Hosea, God warned the people of Israel that judgement was near. In the same eternal love, God uses Hosea's words to warn us – urging one and all,

> *"Come let us return to the* LORD*. He has torn us to pieces but he will heal us; he has injured us but he will bind up our wounds. After two days he will revive us; on the third day he will restore us, that we may live in his presence. Let us acknowledge the* LORD*; let us press on to acknowledge him. As surely as the sun rises, he will appear; he will come to us like the winter rains, like the spring rains that water the earth."*   (6:1–3)

We would be wise to heed the warning of Hosea. God hated the sins of the Israelites and brought judgement upon them. He still hates sin and He will judge it. Unless we pay attention to the danger signals in our nations and turn back to God in repentance, we will pay the full, terrifying price for our sins.

Questions to consider

▶ Are you weak and unfulfilled, driven by many forces to the next exciting event or the next purchase?

▶ Are you deceived by lies about love? Is your mind clouded by lust?

▶ In what areas has our society exchanged the truth of God for a lie?

▶ In what areas have you exchanged the truth of God for a lie?

▶ Are you holding to your word and keeping your promises?

▶ Is society ignoring God's warnings?

Remember
Knowing the truth will set you free.

Notes

1. John Bright, *A History of Israel* (London: SCM Press Ltd, 1982), pp. 253–264 and John Marsh, *Amos and Micah* (London: SCM Press Ltd, 1976), pp. 25–26.
2. Extracts from a talk by Dr Jonathan Sacks, the Chief Rabbi, to the Religion and Welfare Conference on 22nd June 2000.
3. Tear Fund information and discussion paper, "Globalisation and the Poor", as cited in the Cafod briefing on globalisation.
4. Bureau of Justice Statistics, "Sexual Assault of Young Children as Reported to Law Enforcement: Victim, Incident, and Offender Characteristics".
5. *The Telegraph*, 'One third of clergy do not believe in the resurrection', 31/07/02, at www.telegraph.co.uk/news/main.jhtml?xml=news/2002/07/31/ncreed ... /ixhome.htm
6. Eugene Peterson, *The Message*, "The Old Testament Prophets" (Colorado Springs: Navpress, 2000), p. 436.
7. *Chambers 21st Century Dictionary* (1999).
8. Dawson McAllister at http://christiananswers.net/-dml/dml-y030.html
9. http://www.geocities.com/me2kangaru/Cassie.html

JOEL
(850–810 BC)

~∽ ∾~

Chapter 2

Wrong Questions = Wrong Answers

*"The trouble with our age is
that it is all signpost and no destination."*
(Louis Kronenberger)

Famine was in the land. Acres of precious crops had fallen prey to plagues of locusts. The locusts advanced year after year like a wildfire, incinerating everything in their path. The land and crops were destroyed. The Israelite agricultural economy was in tatters. It was a national catastrophe. Poverty was rife. The people were destitute, lacking even the basics for survival.

Joel describes their dark and dismal predicament with these words,

"Has not the food been cut off before our very eyes – joy and gladness from the house of our God? The seeds are shrivelled beneath the clods. The storehouses are in ruins, the granaries have been broken down for the grain has dried up. How the cattle moan! The herds mill about because they have no pasture; even the flocks of sheep are suffering." (1:16–18)

When disaster strikes, it shakes the foundations of who we are and what we believe. Some are frozen by fear, unable to think or act – their faces masked with terror. Some deny the seriousness of the situation. Some blame God. Others plan and scheme to circumvent the problem. Still others are short-sighted, blinded by their vanity to the reality of God's judgement. They say, "God is with us, everything will work out alright."

So often in a crisis we look for scapegoats, things or people to blame, rather than taking personal responsibility and facing the issues, both natural and spiritual, and then taking the appropriate action. When disaster strikes, our understanding of God often becomes distorted. Whether flood or drought, unforeseen death or illness, national calamity or personal loss, disaster causes many people to point the finger at God and make accusations: "God is unjust", "God is angry", "God is absent".

Into such a scene of destruction and misunderstanding God sent Joel, His crisis counsellor, to bring men and women "to an immediate awareness that there wasn't a day that went by that they weren't dealing with God."[1] Joel's message has application at every level of life, from the unanswerable questions that surround the tragic death of a young child to momentous national and international disasters.

Joel's challenge to the people of Israel is equally applicable to you and me. Are we going to attribute blame or take responsibility? Are we going to make outrageous accusations against God or deal with our part of the problem? Joel's first suggestion to the Israelites was not about pesticide or better farming methods. It was not to repair the damaged land and to sow seed again. His first suggestion is spiritual, calling one and all to come back to God in sorrow and repentance. Calling the priests, the ministers, the elders and *"all who live in the land to the house of the* LORD *your God ... to cry out to the* LORD*"* (1:14). Blow a trumpet, sound an alarm (2:1) he urges them, as he describes the woeful calamity that the occupying army of locusts have and are exacting on the land and nation.

There is an urgency in his tone which is not hard to imagine. Before his very eyes the locusts are marching, a multimillion-member marauding army wreaking havoc. *"Even now,"* he says on God's behalf, *"return to me with all your heart with fasting and weeping and mourning. Rend your heart and not your garments. Return to the* LORD *your God"* (2:12–13). It is language of deep penitence and remorse driving the Israelites out of their self-centred independence from God and their persistent disobedience of His invaluable instructions. As Joel calls the nations to repentance he recalls the other side of God's love for the people: *"for he is gracious and compassionate, slow to anger and rich in love, and he relents from sending calamity. Who knows? He may turn and have pity and leave behind a blessing"* (2:13–14).

Joel confirms the necessity and importance of the nation's repentance by repeating the call, pleading for action to be taken. *"Declare a holy fast, call a sacred assembly. Gather the people, consecrate the assembly"* (2:15–16). But who should attend? Not just the leaders and elders, but everyone, children, breast-feeding mothers and even the bride and groom should be invited to attend from their honeymoon bed! All are to agree and intercede with God, *"Spare your people, O LORD. Do not make your inheritance an object of scorn, a byword among the nations. Why should they say among the peoples, 'Where is their God?'"* (2:17).

How would God, gracious and compassionate, slow to anger and rich in love, respond to the Israelites' demonstration of heartfelt contrition and repentance? Here's how: God speaks through Joel declaring that He would transform their desperate circumstances, *"I am sending you grain, new wine and oil, enough to satisfy you fully"* (2:19). *". . . I will drive the northern army far from you, pushing it into a parched and barren land"* (2:20). *". . . I will repay you for the years the locusts have eaten"* (2:25). *". . . I will pour out my spirit on all people"* (2:28). *". . . I will show wonders in the heavens and on the earth"* (2:30).

The third and final chapter contains a further awesome promise. God promises to restore the nation's fortunes; all that had been lost to the locusts due to the Israelites' sinful lifestyle would be restored by God (3:1). Repentance, returning and renewing of hearts will lead to fortunes being restored by God. What a liberating truth! Having used catastrophe to gain the peoples' attention and catalyse a change in attitude and worship, the prophecy focuses on the surrounding nations, nations who have delighted in Israel's downfall, speeding it along by their ill-treatment of this downtrodden nation.

God reveals that their actions had not gone unnoticed and

that the time for retribution was at hand: *"You took my silver and my gold and carried off my finest treasures to your temples. You sold the people of Judah ... that you might send them far from their homeland ... I will return on your own heads what you have done"* (3:5–7). A tremendous judgement on the nations is foretold as the language of war and armies returns to Joel's prophecy (3:9–16). In a final flourish Israel's tormentors, Egypt and Edom are condemned, and in sweet and poetic language God's favour is spoken over Israel and her people (3:17–21).

Do any of Joel's words and warnings have relevance today? Are there any lessons to learn from how we deal with catastrophe, disaster and the hard and unanswerable questions of life? I think there are.

Why does God allow people to suffer catastrophes and disasters? Certainly a difficult question, but not an opportunity to adopt the hazardous misconception of holding God responsible for all the troubles in the world. God is a God whose love knows no limit; He never stops loving. If His people aren't experiencing His blessing, if they've suffered a crushing blow, He may be trying to say something.

Understanding what He is saying often requires revelation, an ability to see the unseen, before we can grasp the wider implications of contemporary events or see the wider canvas of God's ultimate purpose and intention in our lives and our societies. I don't mean to suggest, however, that all will be made crystal clear by divine revelation. God is not committed to showing us everything: *"The secret things belong to the LORD our God, but the things revealed belong to us and to our children for ever"* (Deuteronomy 29:29).

We will not always be able to see God's blueprints laid out before us in their entirety. Instead we must exercise our faith, and trust that God loves us as a father loves his child – His plan for our lives is perfectly designed for our benefit, our wellbeing and our development. We should seek comfort in the wonderful and reassuring truth that God has a master plan that is bigger and grander than ours.

"Who can I blame?" Other people may have some responsibility for the catastrophes that occur in our lives, but looking for someone to blame will not and does not solve the problem. I have encountered too many people in my life who are living unfulfilling lives – people with unrealised dreams; unreleased from failure to move on and close painful chapters. They still blame God and hold grudges. They are unforgiving and bitter towards other members of the human race. They fail to realise that their reaction to past difficulty is limiting the development of their life today.

In counselling, people talk about the "presenting problem". Training enables experts to see beyond the immediate issues to the underlying, fundamental difficulty. Joel's message teaches us, whether in our personal life or in our relationships with others, that we need to find the spiritual key as a prerequisite to unlocking the cause of the physical event. The locusts were not the Israelites' root problem; simply a product of their poor spiritual condition.

So often we attempt solutions based around the practical issues of a problem. I don't deny that this is necessary, but it must not come before or in substitution for facing the deeper moral, relational and spiritual realities.

Like the ancient nation of Israel, the Western world has some huge lessons to learn about this principle. Governments and agencies spend mountains of money, put to work the best brains available, and urgently seek for capable and energetic people – all in an attempt to resolve the seemingly intractable and persistent problems associated with modern urban communities. Whether it is in health care, education, law and order, the impoverished housing estates or any other of the numerous topics that dominate the political agenda, we seem to be fighting a losing battle, struggling to make meaningful and tangible progress. I am convinced that until we give proper priority to the spiritual, relational and moral issues that lie at the roots of all the issues of our day, we can only expect meagre success.

We ignore God and disobey His laws. We are arrogant to the point of believing we are self-sufficient, that science and economics will eventually solve all our problems. We are arrogant to the point of believing that we are accountable to no power greater than ourselves. But science or any other part of our pool of human genius cannot deliver all the other essential ingredients for a fulfilled life. The exercise of King Solomon's wisdom in the famous case of the disputed baby demonstrates this truth.

Two women came to Solomon seeking "justice" (1 Kings 3:16–28). Each woman had recently given birth to a son. When one of the babies died in the night, the mother switched his body with the other woman's living baby. Both now claimed that the living baby was theirs. Solomon cleverly cut through the conflicting claims in this way: he ordered that a sword be brought to the court and offered to give each mother half of the disputed child. As Solomon had hoped, the real mother cried out, relinquishing her claim in order to spare her child's life.

The real mother understood that although in mathematics half plus a half makes one, two halves of a human cannot make one life. Conversely, I have two children. My wife, Dorothy and I do not give half our love to each child; we give both of them all of our love. There is something about our humanity that is more than science can or ever will be able to explain. We are amazing and wonderful machines, but we are also much more: we are moral, relational and ultimately spiritual beings who can never be complete and at peace with ourselves until we are at peace with others. And we will never be fully at peace with others until we are at peace with God.

Consider: how can a passionless school assembly, conducted with religious content, often only because the law requires it, involving some bland teaching on citizenship, prepare the deep and foundational spirituality that each child needs to become a fully developed human being? How can a curriculum, however brilliantly taught, that is constructed without a serious moral, relational and spiritual foundation prepare our children to live as full and complete human beings? We need, as the people of Israel did in Joel's day, to repent and change our ways of thinking and living. The locusts are devouring our land, destroying our young people and we continue in our deluded ways insisting everything will be all right in the end.

A study on school children in the UK found that 49.3% of boys and 37.4% of girls aged 15–16 years admitted having stolen items in the past.[2]

In the US half of all 13–17 year olds have had sexual intercourse[3] ... 863,000 teen girls became pregnant in the US in 1997[4] ... approximately one in four sexually active teens in the US gets a STD every year.[5]

In 1999 a study on US college students revealed that 44.1% of males and 22.7% of females were "binge" drinking.[6]

In schools throughout the world, the myth of evolution is taught and perpetuated – an unproven theory that lays down an accidental existence. We hold on to the idea that our first reason for living is to help the human race reach the next generation, but we're not quite sure of the ultimate destination. Our children are taught that nobody created the world – it just happened – a big bang! Why are we surprised that these same young people have no great sense of self-worth or personal value? Why are we surprised that many are selfish, living only for pleasure, lacking any great dream or purpose in life? We have robbed them of a godly spiritual dimension, we teach them to be less than they are, rather than encouraging them to be all that God designed them for.

"The scientist's religious feeling takes the form of a rapturous amazement at the harmony of natural law, which reveals an intelligence of such superiority that, compared with it, all the systematic thinking and acting of human beings is an utterly insignificant reflection."[7]

Professor Albert Einstein

> **Impossible odds:**
> Eminent scientists Dr Francis Crick and Dr Carl Sagan estimated that the difficulty of evolving a man by chance process alone is 1 in 10 followed by 2 billion zeroes! Those zeroes would fill approximately ten thousand books containing 150 pages![8]

This loss of direction is not a recent phenomenon. It's been smouldering away for a considerable number of years. Many of our culture's great icons, raised with a worldview devoid of purpose, have expressed the futility of this philosophy. Consider the lyrics the rock group Queen sang in 1991:

> Empty spaces – what are we living for
> Abandoned places – I guess we know the score
> On and on, does anybody know what we are looking
>   for...
> Another hero, another mindless crime
> Behind the curtain, in the pantomime
> Hold the line, does anybody want to take it anymore
> The show must go on
> The show must go on, yeah
> Inside my heart is breaking
> My make-up may be flaking
> But my smile still stays on
>
> Whatever happens, I'll leave it all to chance
> Another heartache, another failed romance
> On and on, does anybody know what we are living for?
> I guess I'm learning
> I must be warmer now
> I'll soon be turning
> Round the corner now
> Outside the dawn is breaking
> But inside in the dark I'm aching to be free
> The show must go on, yeah yeah
> Ooh, inside my heart is breaking
> My make-up may be flaking
> But my smile still stays on[9]

If you read these words and feel something stir within that draws you to some brighter horizon of opportunities and possibilities than you currently enjoy, you need to recognise that you are a special, unique creation of God. Whether your parents wanted you or not, God planned your life and gave you all the gifts and abilities required to achieve the purpose He designed you for. Through His son Jesus Christ, God is eager to help you live a purposeful life for His glory, the benefit of society and your fulfilment.

The US has been overcome with grief following a continuing spate of youth gun crime: the Columbine High School shootings in Colorado, to quote one example. But what is the solution? A change in gun laws? The father of one of fifteen victims who died at the hands of two teenage gunmen, said these words to the subcommittee of the US House Judicial Committee.

> "The first recorded act of violence was when Cain slew his brother Abel out in the field. The villain was not the club he used. Neither was it the NCA, the National Club Association. The true killer was Cain, and the reason for the murder could only be found in Cain's heart. In the days that followed the tragedy, I was amazed at how quickly fingers began to be pointed at groups such as the NRA [National Rifle Association]. I am not a member of the NRA. I am not a hunter. I do not even own a gun. I am not here to represent or defend the NRA – because I don't believe that they are responsible for my daughter's death ... I am here today to declare that Columbine was not just a tragedy – it was a spiritual event that should be forcing us to look at where the blame lies! ... I wrote a poem just four nights ago that expresses my feelings best. This was written way before I knew I would be speaking here today:
>
> Your laws ignore our deepest needs,
> Your words are empty air.
> You've stripped away our heritage,
> You've outlawed simple prayer.

Now gunshots fill our classrooms,
And precious children die.
You seek for answers everywhere,
And ask the question 'Why?'

You regulate restrictive laws,
Through legislative creed.
And yet you fail to understand,
That God is what we need!"[10]

We will not solve the problems in our societies by trying to get rid of the "locusts" without first attending to the deeper spiritual issues that lie at the root of Western civilisation's deteriorating social order. Pressurised by a flood of social ills we will persist in asking the wrong questions – examining only the presenting problem rather than dealing with its underlying cause. We will point the finger at unemployment, poverty, drug abuse and family breakdown as the ringleaders in a campaign of crime. We then place our hope in legislation and economics to combat these problems– and we're always disappointed.

A mutually inclusive approach is required. If we deal with the underlying spiritual issues we will gain clearer insight and more energy to tackle the presenting problems as they begin to right themselves, by appropriately directing the legislation or economics as necessary. If we fail to adopt a holistic – spiritually inclusive – view of our societies and ourselves we will continue to ask the wrong questions and apply the wrong solutions.

The hope of Joel's prophecy is that if we ask the right questions we can find the right answers, we will be able to apply our minds correctly and effectively. In short we will visibly see the situation change dramatically.

There are many instances of striking transformations that have occurred when the spiritual agenda has been given its rightful place in society. Perhaps one of the most exciting is the Great Welsh Revival of 1904 – an inspiring illustration of the impact of heartfelt contrition and repentance. The Revival began with the preaching of Evan Roberts and quickly spread from church to church like a tidal wave over Wales. The prominent historian J. Edwin Orr records:

> "The social impact was astounding. For example, judges were presented with white gloves, not a case to try; no robberies, no burglaries, no rapes, no murders, and no embezzlements, nothing. District councils held emergency meetings to discuss what to do with the police now that they were unemployed ... As the revival swept Wales, drunkenness was cut in half. There was a wave of bankruptcies, but nearly all taverns. There was even a slow down in the mines, for so many Welsh coal miners were converted and stopped using bad language that the horses that dragged the coal trucks in the mines could not understand what was being said to them."[11]

The time for action is now. There can be no delay. Tomorrow never comes, memories fade, the situation snowballs and the problems get worse. In my office, I have the words "Carpe Diem – Seize the Day" embroidered in a picture frame on my wall. It serves as a constant reminder to me to that procrastination is not only the thief of time, it is also the grave of opportunity.[12] Like the Israelite nation, the West needs to act now, to seize the day and return to God with all its heart to put an end to many of the painful problems of our societies.

My heart races at the mere thought of the promised outpouring of the Holy Spirit on all people (2:28). God promised the Israelites grain, wine and oil, a very welcome gift to a destitute and starving nation. But He also promised them much more, His Spirit – the breath of God. There's an important lesson to learn here. However tempted we may be to remain where we are when our immediate physical needs are met, we must press on to experience the deeper things of God.

To help us to understand what this promise means we must travel forward in time, eight hundred and fifty years or so, to the early Christian Church on the day of Pentecost, seven weeks after Jesus' crucifixion. On this day, Peter quoted Joel's prophecy (2:28–32) to express the strange events which were taking place.

> *"Suddenly a sound like a blowing of violent wind came from heaven and filled the whole house where they were sitting. They saw what seemed to be tongues of fire that separated and came to rest on each of them. All were filled with the Holy Spirit and began to speak in other languages as the Spirit enabled."*
>
> (Acts 2:2–4)

This is a new stage in the revelation of God to all people, where a fuller immersion or baptism in the Holy Spirit, a greater level of continued access to the Holy Spirit, was made available through the cleansing power of Jesus Christ's death.

What is the effect of this blessing? Joel indicates that it brings a fuller experience of God, enabling people to prophesy, dream dreams and see visions (2:28). The Holy Spirit empowers Christians to live holy lives and bestows divine gifts on believers for the benefit of the world.

The power of Pentecost is revolutionary. Two thousand years ago, the first recipients of this promise turned their world upside down and penetrated their culture, giving humankind a hope for a better, more dynamic way of living. Our societies, like the human body need all the right parts to function effectively. But we also need breath, because if all we've got is a brain and a body, we expire. We need to experience the breath of God; its inspiration breathing a new dimension of life to our societies.

The Spirit's power – this new dimension – is still available. It was available then and it is available now. The door has never been closed. William Booth, the founder of the Salvation Army wrote, "We want another Pentecost". Although I understand the sentiment and emotion he was trying to convey – a desire to experience the fullness of the Holy Spirit – we do not need to wait for another Pentecost. Pentecost is alive today. We must earnestly embrace its power. Echoing the words of John Wesley, we must allow God to set us on fire so the people of the world can watch us burn.

Throughout the Christian era this spirituality, exhibiting the empowering gift of the Holy Spirit, surfaced only erratically until the beginning of the twentieth century, when the present Pentecostal movement began. In the past century it has swept to all quarters of the earth. Western civilisation would be wise to take more notice of these developments, for, as Joel says, they are the indicators of what is to come. These events herald *"the coming of the great and dreadful day of the LORD"* (2:31) (see chapter 4).

It is fascinating that whilst much of Western journalism would offer an obituary for the death of Christianity, more people enjoy a personal experience of Jesus Christ through repentance, faith and forgiveness than history has ever known. Hundreds of millions of these people enjoy the fulfilment of Joel's words, experiencing the Holy Spirit in profound and supernatural ways.

> The Pentecostal/Charismatic movement is the fastest growing religion in the world, growing by 7.3% each year. It is estimated that there are 553 million Pentecostals/Charismatics world-wide.[13]

Throughout history many false prophets – great philosophers – have mistakenly predicted the downfall of Christianity. The French intellectual Voltaire, a shining light during the period referred to as the Enlightenment, "boasted that in one hundred years Christianity would be a museum piece. Infidelity ran riot in France. Voltaire, however, passed screaming into eternity, but the Bible has not passed away. Moreover, Voltaire's printing press was used to print the very Scriptures which he boasted he had demolished and his house became a depot for the Geneva Bible Society."[14]

As we march into the new millennium, our nations wounded by corporate catastrophes and our fellow citizens suffering personal disasters, will we listen to Joel? Or will his call to repentance fall on deaf ears? I leave you with these final words of warning:

> *"Because of your stubbornness and your unrepentant heart, you are storing up wrath against yourself for the day of God's wrath, when his righteous judgement will be revealed. God 'will give to each person according to what he has done.'"*   (Romans 2:5–6)

Questions to consider

- ▶ Have the struggles of life made you bitter or better?

- ▶ Are you pointing the finger, dealing with difficulty by blaming God or by blaming others?

- ▶ Have you asked God to reveal something of the bigger picture beyond your present circumstances?

- ▶ Are you earnestly seeking to experience the deeper things of God?

- ▶ Is the Western world asking the wrong questions about our social ills?

- ▶ Are you running on the hamster wheel – tired, hopeless and desperate?

Remember
*Wisdom asks the right questions and
God gives His Holy Spirit to those who ask Him.*

Notes

1. Eugene Peterson, *The Message*, "The Old Testament Prophets" (Colorado Springs: Navpress, 2000), p. 462.
2. Cited in "Risk and protective factors associated with youth crime and effective interventions to prevent it", Youth Justice Board Research Note No. 5, Youth Justice Board, 2001 (found at www.nacro.org.uk/data/briefings/nacro-200230100–ycs.pdf).
3. The Centres for Disease Control and Prevention, Youth Risk Behaviour Trends, from Youth Behaviour Survey, 1999, from Kaiser Family Foundation at www.kff.org/content/2001/20011211a/TeenSexualActivity.pdf

4. The Centres for Disease Control and Prevention, National state-specific pregnancy rates among adolescents – United States, 1995–1997, Morbidity and Mortality Weekly Report, July 2000, 49(27), from Kaiser Family Foundation at www.kff.org/content/2001/20011211a/ TeenSexualActivity.pdf
5. The Alan Guttmacher Institute, *Sex and America's Teenagers* (New York, 1994), p. 38.
6. Bureau of Justice Statistics, *Sourcebook of Criminal Justice Statistics Online*, Section 3 "Nature and distribution of known offences", Table 3.83, p. 256, at www.albany.edu/sourcebook/1995/pdf/section3.pdf
7. From *The World As I See It*, (Watts & Co.), p. 9.
8. www.homepages.at/slush/evol – Carl Sagan, F.H.C. Crick and L.M. Mukhin in Carl Sagan (ed.), *Communication with Extraterrestrial Intelligence (CETI)* (Cambridge, MA: MIT Press, 1973), pp. 45–46; cf. Emile Borel, *Probabilities and Life* (New York: Dover, 1962), chapters 1 and 3.
9. http://www.queenwords.com/lyrics/songs/sng19_16.shtml
10. Dated: 27th May 1999, at www.house.gov/judiciary/scot0527.pdf
11. From article based on one of Edwin Orr's messages at www.revival-library.org/catalogues/prayer/orr/index.html or J. Edwin Orr, *The Flaming Tongue: The Impact of Twentieth-Century Revivals* (Chicago: Moody Press, 1973), pp. 17–18.
12. Anonymous quote, www.ucalgary.ca/~steel/procrastinus/quotes.html
13. Reference: International Bulletin of Missionary Research, January 2003. David B. Barrett and Todd M. Johnston.
14. Ian Paisley, *Christian Foundations* (1971) (uncopyrighted) an extract at http://www.whatsaiththescripture.com/The.Holy.Bible/ Reasons7.Bible.Word.of.GOD.html

Chapter 3

Hypocrites Exposed

"He who allows oppression shares the crime."
(Desiderius Erasmus)

The kingdom of Israel, under the rule of King Jeroboam II had risen to the pinnacle of her prosperity. Prosperity unlocked the door to a house full of vice, a house that stank of moral rottenness. Israel liberated and reclaimed her lost territories as the surrounding empires declined in power and influence. A new wave of multiculturalism crashed onto her shores, carrying inanimate objects floating in a sea of shadowy gods. This sea would water the roots of deception, encouraging the Israelites to become a people who were bold and shameless in their willingness to pursue false religions.

It was a time of dramatic social change, predominantly brought about by the "the cynical opportunism of the *nouveaux riches* in expropriating the small peasant farmer whenever occasion presented itself, as it would, for instance in a year of bad or mutilated harvest. The Israel that Amos came to know was thus a state where large fortunes were being quickly made, great estates being developed, summer houses and winter residences being built in fabulous luxury for the wealthy, and where, at the same time, there was quite a new class of poor, who were virtually, and sometimes actually, slaves of their rich landlords."[1]

God called Amos, a country-farmer with no political allegiances, from obscurity "in a final effort to stay the nation from its mad dash for death."[2] He stirred Amos to remind the people that He cannot condone injustice or accept religious hypocrisy.

Amos was neither accredited nor trained as a prophet. He was an ordinary yet capable person who was well aware of the political and religious affairs of the nations. As a contemporary of Hosea he spoke out God's righteous anger against a nation of self-centred pleasure seekers. Through Amos, God reveals His sovereignty over all nations; even nations that worshipped other gods were accountable to Him and under His control.

So what did this simple shepherd have to say? Amos' message begins with a dramatic description of the impending destruction of a host of nations for their many sins. Each indictment is drawn up in the same terms, "For three sins ... even for four, I will not turn back my wrath." The numbers are used in contrast to one or two – a few – to indicate a variety of many sins; a broken threshold which pleaded for judgement. This time they had gone too far, and judgement was coming.

Each indictment names a specific sin, a hallmark of the depth of the nation's evil ways. The first indictment is read out by Amos against Damascus, a people castigated for their excessive cruelty (1:3). Second is the Philistine nation and in particular the city of Gaza, a city condemned for taking captive and selling whole communities, not just soldiers captured in battle (1:6). Amos moves his attention north from Gaza to Tyre, the Phoenician merchant city, allied to Israel by an ancient binding treaty of friendship (1 Kings 5:1–12). Tyre is denounced for profiting from the slave trade; selling communities of captured Israelites in direct contravention of a binding international agreement (1:9). The Southern nation of Edom is next condemned for pursuing *"his brother with a sword, stifling all compassion"* (1:11). The Eastern province of Ammon is censured for wretched cruelty driven by greed for land: *"he ripped open the pregnant women of Gilead in order to extend his borders"* (1:13). No one would be allowed to stand in the way of the Ammonites' insatiable desire, least of all the unborn child who could lay no claim to his rightful inheritance. Finally Moab, the last of the foreign nations, is denounced for violent and vindictive hatred (2:1).

Each indictment is an account for which there can be no defence. The evidence is insurmountable and the verdict is guilty. A penalty must be issued. Amos therefore delivers God's sentence, depicting destruction and ruin. He describes palaces, fortresses and nations consumed by fire, cities crushed, people exiled and kings slain.

Sadly, Amos has more to say. He points the finger at Judah, his home nation, for rejecting God's laws by being seduced by false gods (2:4). And lastly, Israel is condemned for crimes of oppression, corruption and desecration (2:6–8).

The Israelites are unmasked as a people wilfully defiant of justice, living off ill-gotten gains. No mercy or favouritism remains for Israel, a nation that boasts an amazing history of God-given deliverance and leadership. On the contrary, special privilege gives rise to special responsibility – which demands greater condemnation from a just God when responsibilities are neglected. The Israelites' fate was to be more severe than that of their neighbours. God's anger had been roused and He stirred Amos to speak out His judgement against Israel, from which there would be no escape (2:13–16).

Again, history records that what God said came to pass. The Assyrians destroyed the Northern Kingdom of Israel in 722 BC, deporting and torturing thousands of captured Israelites. With the exclusion of Edom, which was conquered by the Nabatean Arabs in the fifth century BC, the remaining six nations condemned in Amos' prophecy were destroyed during the forty-three year rule of King Nebuchadnezzar, ruler of the Babylonian Empire between 604–562 BC.[3]

As for the remainder of the book, chapters 3 to 6 are a series of judgements, most notably judgement on self-indulgent people who have accumulated their wealth by oppression (chapter 4) and judgement on false religion. Chapters 7 to 9 contain five pictures revealed by God to Amos depicting the phases of Israel's progression towards judgement:

- Phase 1: *"The sovereign LORD showed me: He was preparing swarms of locusts"* (7:1). We have seen from the book of Joel that locusts are used in these settings as a judgement from God. Amos pleaded with God, *"Forgive!"* (7:2) And God relented.

- Phase 2: *"The sovereign* LORD *was calling for judgement by fire; it dried up the great deep and devoured the land"* (7:4). Seeing what God was doing Amos cried out, *"Sovereign* LORD, *I beg you, stop . . . "* (7:5) and God relented for a second time.

- Phase 3: *"What do you see, Amos?"* God said. *"A plumb-line,"* Amos replied. *"Then the* LORD *said, 'Look I am setting a plumb-line among my people Israel; I will spare them no longer' "* (7:8). The plumb-line is a well-known builder's tool, a device to determine whether what is being built is straight or crooked; a device which cannot of itself build straight walls. God gave the Israelites the ultimate plumb-line – His laws – to instruct and guide them, but they were not building straight walls, so God decreed that it was time for Him to act.

- Phase 4: the Sovereign Lord showed Amos a basket of ripe fruit and said, *"The time is ripe for my people Israel; I will spare them no longer"* (8:2).

- Phase 5: finally, Amos saw the Lord standing by an altar. Throughout Old Testament history, the altar is the place where God's judgement is met by His mercy. The ultimate love statement of the universe is Jesus on the cross, God's final altar where His complete judgement of all man's sin is met by His mercy. The blood of a perfect sacrifice – Jesus Christ – pays the penalty price for sin and offers freedom for all. Amos, however, is looking upon a broken and neglected altar, where mercy has no home. God was about to commence the destruction, to balance the scales of justice, from the very place the Israelites would expect to hear words of peace and blessing. This final picture reveals a God of love, justice and mercy who is left with only one option, judgement.

In the midst of judgement we must remember that God is a

God who keeps His promises, who causes His love eventually to triumph. In the final five verses of the book, the kind and compassionate nature of God is revealed. God promises restoration after judgement (9:11–15). This theme runs throughout the Old Testament speaking of restored ruins, repaired cities, a land rich with ripe fruit, and a time of great blessing and favour.

The passage of time has provided a fuller understanding of the amazing depths and true significance of God's promise to restore Israel. To whom was God promising restoration? Was God's promise limited to providing for physical needs? In the infancy of the Christian church, (Acts 15:16–17), an argument broke out about who could be saved by Jesus' sacrifice: was circumcision, a seal of righteousness stipulated in the Old Testament, required for salvation? The argument was resolved by James, Jesus' half-brother, quoting Amos' prophecy (9:11–12). James used these verses as a platform to unite the Jews with all non-Jews, demonstrating that it has always been God's intention to restore (or save) every man, woman and child of every race without distinction or favour. The legalistic requirement of circumcision could never be a barrier to salvation; it is fulfilled by faith in the sacrifice of Jesus Christ, who pours out righteousness on all who believe.

Imagine a world summit where every leader from the four corners of the earth is called to be in attendance. Amos is the main speaker – what would he say? Would he be issuing indictments and condemning nations? I believe he would.

The Western nations do not have clean hands: we engage in arms-length bombing campaigns, describing civilian casualties as "collateral damage". We oppress the poor to sustain our comfortable lifestyles. We break binding treaties to protect our own interests. We are by no means alone in our iniquity; as most of us are aware, brutal atrocities are happening in Afghanistan, Burma, North Korea, Sudan and many other places in the world. God is watching. He cannot turn a blind eye to what He sees. Can you see what we're storing up for ourselves?

In 1999 the United Nations estimate that there were **20 million** adult bonded labourers (i.e. **slaves**) world-wide.[4]

Based on reliable estimates, 700,000 to 2 million people, particularly women and children, are trafficked each year across international borders. Victims of trafficking are **forced** to toil under horrific conditions in sweatshops and on construction sites, in fields and brothels.[5]

Every year one million children are **exploited** by people or circumstances to enter the sex trade.[6]

The prosperity of Israel's wealthy depended on oppression and robbery. *"They sell the righteous for silver, and the needy for a pair of sandals. They trample on the heads of the poor as upon the dust of the ground and deny justice to the oppressed ... In the house of their god they drink wine taken as fines ... You trample on the poor and force him to give you grain."* (2:6–8; 5:11). It is a painfully familiar story.

Like Israel's wealthy, a substantial proportion of the West's prosperity is dependent upon oppression. We are complicit in a culture that protects itself at the expense and deprivation of others. We trample on the heads of the poor as if they were dust on the ground. We, like the Israelites, have been given a plumb-line – God's ancient and just laws – but we have chosen to disregard them. In our arrogance, we have exchanged the laws of God for the laws of man. We have not resisted this greedy, self-seeking, self-justifying society.

It is time for us to face the truth, to look deep into the mirror and face our own reflection – the guilty image of evil extortioners. We do not need to look far for evidence to illustrate our crimes: "The International Monetary Fund (IMF), which has blocked more substantial debt cancellation, is controlled by the voting power of its members. The G8 countries [the eight largest developed countries in the world, including the US and the UK] control 48 per cent of the votes; the 41 Heavily Indebted Poor Countries (HIPCs) have only 3 per cent. If the votes were allocated on the basis of population rather than level of financial contribution to the IMF, the G8 would have 14 per cent in comparison to the HIPC countries 10 per cent."[7]

Many high street brands continue to capitalise on the doctrine of justified oppression that pervades Western society. The trademarks of injustice are stamped on our clothes and most of us wear them with pride. Battery farms of humans toil hard in sweatshops to keep our faces smiling – working in conditions of extreme exploitation, including the absence of a living wage or benefits, poor working conditions and arbitrary discipline, such as verbal and physical abuse.

Oppression doesn't end with the global garment business. The next time you bite into a banana or drink a cup of coffee consider the working conditions which were endured for your benefit: long hours, low pay, forced overtime, massive exposure to dangerous pesticides and lack of job security.

There's no doubt about it: we're all guilty. We cannot claim fair play and wash our hands of our responsibilities to the many millions we've trampled under foot. There will be a reckoning for our behaviour – we will receive our just deserts. We may be offended by the inclusiveness of the "we" – that we share in the crimes of our countries – but we must rise to the

---

A Nike quilted jacket costs £100 in a London shop, but only 51p of that goes to the Bangledeshi woman who made it.[8]

The $750 million spent on the Okinawa G7 summit could have written off the entire debts of Ethiopia and the Gambia.[9]

The cost of providing basic health care and nutrition **for all** would be less than is spent in Europe and the US on **pet food**.[10]

For every £1 in aid granted to developing countries, more than £13 comes back in debt repayments.[11]

If debt had been cancelled in 1997 for twenty of the poorest countries, the money released for basic healthcare could have **saved the lives** of about 21 million children by the year 2000, the equivalent of **19,000 children a day**.[12]

challenge and play our part in mitigating these and other societal sins.

Our world is full of a multitude of different religions; each in the wrong hands can be manipulated to justify the commission of the most horrific crimes. The history of misguided religious belief has left its scars in every civilisation, from the crusades of the Middle Ages to Islamic fundamentalist groups of today. There has not been a moment in history when "religion re-written" was not creating bloodshed. Is there a hope for religion? Should we give up on religion all together? To answer these questions we must look to the prophets of the Old Testament, for "The biblical prophets continue to be the most powerful and effective voices ever heard on this earth for keeping religion honest, humble and compassionate."[13]

Amos spoke out against the Israelites' religious hypocrisy. *"Bring your sacrifices every morning, your tithes every three years. Burn leavened bread as a thank-offering and brag about your freewill offerings – boast about them, you Israelites, for this is what you love to do"* (4:4–5). The word "hypocrisy" stems from the Greek word, *hypokrisia*, which means, "acting or playing a part". A modern dictionary definition reads, "the act of pretending to have feelings, beliefs or principles which one does not actually have ... the act of concealing one's true character."[14]

The Israelites were acting a part – they were not sincere. They made offerings and sacrifices and paid their tithes, yet life was unrewarding and empty, for, as God said, *"You have not returned to me"* (4:6). *"I hate and despise your religious feasts; I cannot stand your religious assemblies. Even though you bring me burnt offerings and grain offerings, I will not accept them ... Away with the noise of your songs! I will not listen to the music of your harps"* (6:21–23). Like any meaningful relationship, God requires genuine, heart-felt love and obedience. He cannot accept empty praise and insincere offerings.

Don't for a moment think that Amos' words do not ring true for the Christian community. His words are a warning against the vain repetition and outward observation that has hampered Christianity. Ritual observance, liturgical or otherwise is not true Christian faith. Christianity is not about ritual but about relationship. It is Christ in you – the hope of glory – a daily walk of loving obedience, a growing relationship with a living God. It is not a dead cultural construct, a man-made control device which may provide some intellectual pleasures but fails to discover the depths of the power of the gospel. On offer is the joy of living out a relationship with God. Take heed, for the Western world we know was born from this very heritage – genuine Christianity. It cannot be sustained with anything less.

We must not allow ourselves to become complacent, to be seduced by lies so that we no longer practice what we profess. We must act out what we truly believe. If we allow ourselves to fall away from true worship of God, we will become vulnerable to the forces of sin – we can even become instruments of evil. Perhaps you think I'm being melodramatic, using a touch of hyperbole to make point? In 1994 in Rwanda, in the heart of Africa, in a nation that was heralded as predominantly Christian, ten thousand people were murdered every day for one hundred days. Consider the words of Gary Haugen, a United Nations investigator writing from his first-hand experience of the genocide:

> "We should be under no illusions about what exists at the human core. Perfectly ordinary human beings are actually capable of being mass murderers. In Rwanda (to say nothing of Eastern Europe during the Holocaust), the killing was not performed by specially trained pathological killers but ordinary people. When all restraints are released, farmers, clerks, school principals, mothers, doctors, mayors and carpenters can pick up machetes and hack to death defence-less women and children. And this happened to a nation where 80 per cent of the citizens identified themselves as Christian. Unless we wish to cling to racist theories about Africans, or mythologies of education or civilisation (as in

Germany in 1933), we must face the objective, historical facts of the matter. The person without God (or perhaps worse, the person without God, but claiming 'God', 'Jesus', 'Muhammad', whatever) is a very scary creature."[15]

> In the UK in 2000, 60% of the population claimed to belong to a specific religion with 55% being Christian. However, half of all adults aged 18 and over who belonged to a religion have **never** attended a religious service.[16]

Amos informs us of what God is interested in – activity which flows from hearts on fire with love for Him, not simply a heartless, loveless form of religion. Love for God will cause us to appreciate God's creation in ourselves and will lead us to treat all others with dignity and respect, even though we may strongly disagree with certain aspects of their lives. A true love for God simply cannot embrace a regime that seeks to dominate and control. The Christian's duty to evangelise and make disciples (Matthew 28:16–20) is not to coerce others into obedience, but to share God's love with gentleness and respect.

Promising tough times ahead in the midst of economic prosperity, preaching to an expanding, highly optimistic nation, Amos seems to be out of step with his countrymen. He warned the Israelites time and again, *"Seek the LORD and live, or he will sweep through ... like a fire [5:6] ... Seek good, not evil, that you may live. Then the LORD God Almighty will be with you, just as you say he is. Hate evil, love good; maintain justice in the courts. Perhaps the LORD God Almighty will have mercy"* (6:14–15). The Israelites ignored the warning and were destroyed. Will the Western world have the humility to turn back to God? Amos challenged the people, *"Hear this word the LORD has spoken against you,"* (3:1). As he challenged them, he challenges us to hear and obey.

Questions to consider

▶ Do you have a living faith or a formal religion?

▶ Is the Western world guilty of oppression? Are we living off ill-gotten gains?

▶ Should we be better stewards of our significant wealth?

▶ Is idolatry an issue in your life?

▶ Has the gospel restored things to you that you have not yet received?

▶ Should we be concerned that the gap between the rich and the poor is increasing in many countries?

▶ Do we need to change our shopping habits?

Remember
He who lends to the poor gives to God.

Notes

1. John Marsh, *Amos and Micah* (London: SCM Press Ltd, 1976), pp. 25–26.
2. Halley's Bible Handbook (Grand Rapids: Zondervan, 1961).
3. Source: www.chrisitananswers.net/dictionary/
4. ICFTU/Anti Slavery, Forced labour in the 21st century, dec'01, citing UN working group on contemporary forms of slavery, from www.globalmarch.org/worstformsreport/global.html
5. US Dept. of State, Trafficking in Persons Report, July 12, 2001 citing, Secretary Powell and Others, Remarks at Special Briefing Washington, DC, July 12, 2001.
6. World Congress Against Commercial Sexual Exploitation of Children, 27–31 August 1996.
7. IMF website (www.imf.org/external/np/sec/memdir/members.htm), World Health Report 2000 (population for 1999, latest figures) from www.jubilee2000uk.org/databank/usefulstatistics/generalstats.htm
8. Tearfund information and discussion paper, "Globalisation and the Poor", as cited in the Cafod briefing on globalisation.
9. Global Development Finance 2001 – based on total debt stock (EDT) for 1999, latest figures.
10. Compiled by Dr Robinson Rojas (www.rrojadatabank.org/sust2.htm) from Euromonitor 1997, UNDP, UNICEF, UNFPA 1994, HDR 1998, and Research Advisory and Business Intelligence Services 1997.

11. Global Development Finance 2001, based on 1999 figures for grants and total debt repayments.
12. UN Human Development Report, 1997, p. 93.
13. Eugene Peterson, *The Message*, "The Old Testament Prophets" (Colorado Springs: Navpress, 2000), p. 474.
14. *Chambers 21st Century Dictionary* (1999), p. 663.
15. Gary Haugen, *Good News About Injustice* (Inter-Varsity-Press), p. 111.
16. The office of National Statistics (UK), at www.statistics.gov.uk/STATBASE/ssdataset.asp?vlnk=5203

Obadiah
(850–830 BC)[1]

❧❧ ❧❧

Chapter 4

You Reap What You Sow

"From ancient grudge break new mutiny,
Where civil blood makes civil hands unclean."
(William Shakespeare)

Bitterness. No other word could describe it. The rivalry between the Israelites and the Edomites had begun more than a thousand years earlier with the birth of twins – Jacob and Esau (Genesis 25–27). These twins fought and wrestled each other from the moment they were conceived. The brothers were raised and grew up in an environment of favouritism and deception fostered by their parents. Esau, the first born, became a skilful hunter, an earthy man who lusted after the things of the world. Jacob, on the other hand, was a quiet man, a schemer and a plotter who hungered for spiritual power.

Jacob lived up to his name, which means "supplanter" or "deceiver", and tricked his brother into selling his inheritance rights as the oldest son for a single meal. To satisfy his immediate desires, Esau sold his rights to honour and spiritual power for a morsel of food. Jacob's trickery did not end here; assisted by his mother his deceitfulness reached its climax. He tricked his own father, a blind old man, to bestow on himself the blessing his father intended to give to Esau. When Esau discovered his brother's deception his anger boiled over and broke free, turning his bitterness to hatred. *"Esau said in his heart, 'The days of my father are at hand; then I will kill my brother Jacob'"* (Genesis 27:41b).

Esau's anger continued to burn unquenched and accordingly his bitterness took root in the many generations that followed. He became the ancestor of the Edomites who settled in the geographical territory of Mount Seir. They occupied the principal cities of Teman, Bozrah and Petra, the capital of Edom. Jacob, however, became the ancestor – the father – of the twelve tribes of Israel, Edom's neighbours.

National antagonism between the Edomites and the tribes of Jacob, particularly the kingdom of Judah, continued to fester (2 Kings 8:20–22). How would the saga of this family at war finally unfold? Obadiah's prophecy exposes the Edomites' attitude to their brother-nation. The Kingdom of Judah was being invaded (2 Chronicles 21:16–17). The Edomites stood across the fence and watched – glad to see their old relatives and rivals in trouble.

Obadiah's message is a final judgement from God against the Edomites, underlining the truth that eventually you will reap what you sow. Esau brought a curse on his whole family due to his bitter, profane, proud and merciless nature. What Esau sowed, Edom reaped. It is salutary to note that even though the Edomites thought their isolated position was impregnable, the law of sowing and reaping together with the judgement of God destroyed them. The Edomites were displaced from their capital by the Nabatean Arabs, around 500 BC, in fulfilment of Obadiah's prophecy: *"People from the Negev* [the home of the Nabatean Arabs] *will occupy the mountains of Esau"* (verse 19).

In addition to the long-running family feud underpinning Obadiah's message, Obadiah highlights several core objections that provoked God's judgement against the Edomites. If we can understand the Edomites' mistakes, we may learn valuable lessons that will enrich our lives by allowing us to avoid the same errors. Obadiah addresses the Edomites' pride; their indifference; their delight in the misfortune of others; their lack of compassion, characterised in their treatment of refugees; and their profanity.

᷇᷇᷇᷇

It's good to be proud. It's an asset, isn't it? A virtue, not a vice. Pride is society's antidote to insecurity. It is a mass-marketed drug, a sugar-coated pill swallowed to cure our low self-esteem. Pride is our culture's treatment for an endless list of psycho- logical and social problems. We chant the mantra of self- confidence, focusing on our strengths, intellect and wisdom, and dwelling on our achievements and track records. We visit counsellors, psychologists, hypnotists and "lifestyle gurus" in a desperate attempt to reprogram our minds with pride – to believe that we are complete, self-sufficient human beings.

It's not surprising that we falter under this oppressive burden. Caught in a vicious cycle, we raise our self-esteem only to have it shattered under a load we cannot bear alone. Pride twists the truth, inviting us to believe a lie. It steals our confidence away from God, who alone can be trusted, and places it on ourselves. Why would we want to risk skating on thin ice rather than place our confidence in God with whom we can walk on water?

The citizens of Edom were proud. Hidden in the high places in the mountains of Seir, living in cities cut into the rocks, they felt safe and secure. Confident in the security of their stronghold they looked down upon the surrounding nations, boasting, *"Who can bring me down to the ground?"* (verse 3b). The Edomites are described as a soaring eagle, a proud and regal bird, noted for

"There is one vice of which no man in the world is free; which everyone in the world loathes when he sees it in someone else; and of which hardly any people, except Christians ever imagine that they are guilty themselves ... The essential vice, the utmost evil, is pride. Unchastity, anger, greed, drunkenness, and all that, are mere fleabites in comparison: it was through Pride that the devil became the devil; Pride leads to every other vice: it is the complete anti-God state of mind ... As long as you are proud you cannot know God. A proud man is always looking down on things and people; and, of course, as long as you are looking down, you cannot see something that is above you ... "[2]

C.S. Lewis

its strength, keenness of vision and power of flight. How the mighty fall. *"'Though you soar like the eagle and make your nest amongst the stars, from there I will bring you down,' declares the LORD"* (verse 4).

The Edomites' pride deceived them. They were so self-consumed that they were unaware of what was going on around them. They were oblivious to the rising power of the surrounding nations, particularly the Nabatean Arabs, who would burst their inflated egos. Any manifestation of pride will prove costly. Instead, we must cultivate a confidence in God.

The citizens of Edom had ringside seats. From their safe haven high up in the mountains they watched the Philistine and Arab armies attack and invade Judah. How would the Edomites react to the unfolding tragedy that played out before their eyes? Would they stand up for their brother-nation? Would they support and provide assistance to their neighbour? No. The Edomites stood aloof while strangers carried off Judah's wealth and foreigners entered Judah's gates and cast lots for her capital city (verse 11). The Edomites were infected with indifference. They were content in their total lack of concern and interest for their neighbour.

> "The only thing necessary for the triumph of evil
> is for good men to do nothing."
> *Edmund Burke*

Indifference is a rampant virus with an increasing death toll in the Western world. Our hearts have become like stone: dead to the plight of our fellow human beings. Whether spiritually, morally, politically or socially, indifference will exact a high price. In the words of George Bernard Shaw, "The worst sin towards our fellow creatures is not to hate them, but to be indifferent to them: that is the essence of inhumanity." He might be right. A good illustration of our indifference is our attitude to the homeless in our society, poignantly expressed by Phil Collins in his song, *Another Day in Paradise*:

"She called out to the man on the street, 'Sir, can you help
    me?
It's cold and I've nowhere to sleep. Is there somewhere,
    you can tell me?'
He walks on, doesn't look back. He pretends he can't hear
    her.
He starts to whistle as he crosses the street, seems
    embarrassed to be there ... "[3]

The citizens of Edom were also charged with rejoicing and
gloating over Judah's misfortune (verse 12). The Edomites
delighted in the sufferings of others. It may be hard to imagine,
but we too are guilty of this awful accusation. We too love to see
our rivals fall flat on their faces, to look down on our enemies
with an arrogance of supremacy. The Edomites didn't point
the gun, they didn't even load it, but their hearts so rejoiced in
their brother-nation's downfall that they may as well have
pulled the trigger. Sometimes our thoughts alone stand as
sufficient evidence to convict us to a life behind bars, or, dare I
say, worse.

The Edomites didn't just stand, watch and rejoice over the
sufferings of their neighbour. No, this was too good an
opportunity to miss; they looted Judah and seized her wealth
(verse 13). In a world which lives in accordance with the
doctrine of survival of the fittest, are we justified to benefit from
the misfortune of others? Is one man's downfall another man's
gain? Or should we concede in our heart of hearts to a moral law
that prohibits us from profiting from the sufferings of others?

If the Edomites' lack of compassion was not plain to see,
Obadiah made it crystal clear: *"You should not have stood at the
crossroads to cut off those among them who escaped; Nor should you
have delivered up those who remained in the day of distress"* (verse
14). The Edomites erected roadblocks and set ambushes to
prevent the escape of Jerusalem's refugees as they tried to flee
from their oppressors.

So for us the question is: are asylum seekers economic migrants or refugees fleeing persecution? It's a hot topic of debate. Certain sections of the populist press fan the British nation's fears with potentially alarming headlines and articles: "... we resent the scroungers, beggars and crooks who are prepared to cross every country in Europe to reach our generous benefits system";[4] "... illegals flooding into UK ...";[5] "Bogus refugees treated better than UK citizens".[6]

The British aid agency Oxfam have expressed strong concerns about the UK's policies on refugees: "The new system for dealing with applications, while it may be faster, is unlikely to be fairer, not least because applications from some countries, deemed to be safe, will automatically be refused. Other provisions of the act will further marginalise and isolate already vulnerable people ... There are signs of a more sensitive approach on the part of the government. However it still seems that the 1999 [Immigration and Asylum] Act is a crude attempt to deter migration to the UK."[7]

In apparent confirmation of Oxfam's concerns, the *Observer* reports that 150 Zimbabwean asylum seekers were turned back from a British airport in November 2001 and sent straight home to an uncertain but perilous fate.[8] Our attitudes and policies towards refugees need re-examining. We must not, for any reason, neglect the genuine persecuted displaced man or women, boy or girl. In a world where the West has so much, hardhearted self-preservation in this area, it is a sin that will not go unpunished.

The Edomites passionately practised profanity. Their disrespect for God was astounding. They celebrated their neighbour's misfortune by holding a noisy party on God's holy mountain (verse 16b). Their spectacular display of irreverence would leave them with more than a hangover. They were doomed to drink continually from the bitter cup of divine judgement – to drink continually the wrath of God.

Profanity is a popular pastime of many of the citizens of our society. Decade after decade the character, the person, and the reputation of God has been attacked in pandemic proportions. His name is used carelessly without any regard to its awesome significance. His name is used as a curse; as a synonym for expressing unwanted or unpleasant emotions. Could there be any greater contradiction? A name that stands for holiness, righteousness, truth, justice, love, mercy, grace and so much more is used in substitution for offensive four-letter words.

It is the vigour of our culture's lust for profanity that is so alarming. The British media flocked to the steps of a London church to publicise anti-Blasphemy law campaigners reading a blasphemous homoerotic poem. Anti-Blasphemy law campaigners are not alone in the Western world's pursuit of profanity. For example, an "artist" immersed a crucifix in his own urine and the Western world embraced it as "art". It's worth reviewing at this stage the comments made earlier on the consistent campaign in Britain to eradicate the offence of blasphemy. The removal of this foundational law will open the floodgates to yet deeper levels of profanity.

Profanity will reap more than a rotten harvest. The Bible is very clear and consistent in its warning: *"Woe to the wise who call evil good and good evil, who put darkness for light and light for darkness, who put bitter for sweet and sweet for bitter"* (Isaiah 5:20).

"As you have done it shall be done to you" (verse 15), is a simple proven principle: you reap what you sow. Some might mistakenly call it "Karma". Others might recognise it in the words of the Western country singer Willie Nelson: "What goes around, comes around." Maybe we've heard the message, but do we really understand it? What are we sowing? What will we harvest? Are we sowing acts of kindness or selfishness, anger or forgiveness, jealousy or joy?

Make no mistake the target is fixed. This "smart missile" cannot be intercepted, neither can its guidance system be switched off. It will reach its destination. There is only one power that can break the curses on our lives: it is the cross. It requires a commitment to change from us, the authors of our own misfortune. It requires us to face the wrongs of our old ways and to turn from them, and then gives us the opportunity to make a clean start.

How did the Edomites become so profane and devoid of compassion? The dominant answer must lie in the fact that the Edomites inherited the sins of Esau, their father. Esau allowed his jealously and bitterness to grow and fester. It developed a root system and spread throughout his family tree, passing from generation to generation, infecting his descendants and becoming part of their identity.

Our sins don't just hurt ourselves. Ultimately they will damage and destroy the lives of those around us: broken marriages damage children; greed and oppression hamstring nations. It is a self-evident principle – our actions, reactions and our omissions have an impact on the world in which we live. No man or woman is an island. Our choices in every area of life have an impact on other people. The Bible insists that a root of bitterness defiles many people (Hebrews 12:15). We must be careful not to fool ourselves: anyone who maintains a bitter feud cannot control the extent of the damage it will cause – often far beyond the immediate and anticipated circle of influence. Bitterness is unfulfilled revenge; it grows like a cancer until it destroys its victim and the victim's family and friends.

It is essential that we learn how to manage our relationships; to learn how to react to mistrust and misunderstanding without being consumed by our feelings and emotions. With this in mind, can we learn anything from the historical account of Jacob and Esau's savage and long-running personal feud?

After more than twenty years of hiding from his brother, Jacob turned for home to face his enemies within and without. It was time for Jacob to reconcile himself both to his brother and his own reflection. Even starting the journey was difficult. Escaping from Laban, his father-in-law, was a traumatic experience, but after a heated exchange, Jacob broke free from Laban's control and Laban made an agreement with Jacob and let his grand-children and daughters go (Genesis 31:49–50).

As Jacob continued his journey home he sent messengers ahead of him to "sweeten" his brother before their reunion, only to hear that Esau was advancing to meet him with four hundred men. In great fear and distress Jacob divided his possessions and workers into two groups. *"He thought, 'If Esau comes and attacks one group, the group that is left may escape'"* (Genesis 32:8). He prayed, he bargained with God. He strategised into the night pooling his property and family into smaller units, one follow-ing another; it was like a military campaign. Finally, under the cover of darkness, he took his two wives, his two maidservants and his eleven sons, followed by his possessions, and sent them across the stream ahead of him (Genesis 32:22–23). This fear-filled desperate man used all his wit and guile to complete his journey safely. And then, left alone and helpless on the other side of the stream, he met God.

If starting for home was hard, and continuing proved to be a harrowing experience, this finish to the journey, where he met God before meeting his brother, proved to be the night of his life. A Herculean struggle culminated in a defining moment that changed everything. As Jacob wrestled with God, he became aware that his past way of living was unsatisfactory and all that he had acquired was in jeopardy. Thus he fought hard declaring, *"I will not let you go unless you bless me"* (Genesis 32:26).

His cry did not go unanswered. Blessed with a new name, a promise and a limp, he would no longer live a conniving, crafty life as Jacob the deceiver. The sun rose on a new day and a new life. Israel, the prince, looked up into the face of his brother Esau, the chains of his past were broken, the testimony of God's love and kindness was on his lips (Genesis 33:5). A new attitude gripped him (Genesis 33:10) and a future expectation inspired him (Genesis 33:15). He would never look back and he would never be the same.

What about Esau? Forgiving, generous and accepting in the moment of meeting, but not reconciled to change his lifestyle. He married pagan women, and ignored both God and the wishes of his family. His children became the bitter enemies of his brother's offspring. The feud, though temporarily subdued, never ended in Esau's family. Despite the great blessing of material prosperity, his children remained resolute in their spiritual barrenness. And so it continued for generations. The old rivalry rumbled on.

To counter the misunderstandings that plague family life and the unpleasant arguments that cause rifts in our relationships, we should learn from Jacob and Esau. A humility towards God, a supernatural encounter with God, and a trust in and dependence on God made all the difference for Jacob. Esau never had these godly experiences, and although through God's kindness he lived a materially blessed life, he was bitter and resentful. Failing to fulfil the potential of his life he left a poisoned legacy to his family. It could have been so different.

Overcome by awkwardness and embarrassment we often shy away from following in Jacob's footsteps, afraid to make the first step. Fearful of our own reflection, we are content to suppress our emotions. We misguidedly believe that it is better to let sleeping dogs lie.

However, we must be very careful, when attempting to resolve our difficulties, not to effect a quick-fix solution. Patching up our problems with plasters to hide the wounds that lie beneath will be as costly for us as it was for Esau and his family. We must tackle the very heart of the problem.

The benefits of breaking the cycle of bitterness in our lives are as far-reaching as the negative effects of the bitterness itself. We must strive to break free from this vicious cycle that is holding us back and learn to address and forget the painful events of our past. It's time for us to sow a different seed, to permit the situation to change, so that we can reap a different harvest.

How should we live out these principles? At the interpersonal level, the more localised a conflict can stay the better. The parties involved in any misunderstanding, dispute or breakdown of trust can receive grace to remedy the problem. When through gossip or genuine concern and a desire to support, non-essential people become involved, there seems to be a lack of grace for these third parties to resolve or to understand the issues with which they have become entangled. It is wise not to allow these people to become involved in the first place. Jesus gave us the perfect example to follow:

> *"If your brother sins against you, go and show him his fault, just between the two of you. If he listens to you, you have won your brother over. But if he will not listen, take one or two others along, so that 'every matter may be established by the testimony of two or three witnesses.' If he refuses to listen to them, tell it to the church; and if he refuses even the church, treat him as you would a pagan or a tax collector."* (Matthew 18:15–17)

It's worthwhile finishing by briefly examining the life of Esau to consolidate our understanding regarding the righteous principle of retribution in kind. Esau was accused of being a profane man. The New Testament singles him out:

> *"See to it that no-one is ... godless like Esau, who for a single meal sold his inheritance rights as the oldest son. Afterwards, as you know, when he wanted to inherit this blessing, he was rejected. He could bring about no change of mind, though he sought the blessing with tears."* (Hebrews 12:16–17)

Esau's personal behaviour, his profanity, his disregard for holy and precious things reaped in a terrible harvest. A harvest that did not conclude in his unfulfilled lifetime but lingered for centuries, until the final doom of his descendants occurred as foretold in this prophetic book.

How you live can have a profound effect on your children and future generations. This is important to understand. The implications of Esau's lack of respect and profane lifestyle should be remembered when we view contemporary, secular attitudes to all things holy and precious. Profanity is all around us. Millions of people are daily mocking the sacred and ridiculing piety – it's even seen as witty or clever! The Western world has plunged headfirst into a sea of godlessness. In pursuit of our "fix" we satisfy our "now" appetites whatever they are and whomever they may damage. Modern man is sowing his "wild oats". His harvest is surely coming and it won't make pleasant reaping. Remember, *"God is not mocked. A man reaps what he sows"* (Galatians 6:7).

Questions to consider

▶ Is your disobedience damaging the people around you?

▶ Are you practising profanity?

▶ Do you need to sow a different seed?

▶ Are you being deceived by pride?

▶ Are you managing your relationships effectively?

▶ Is there anyone that you have not forgiven?

▶ Are you conscious that the way you live will impact future generations of your family?

Remember
Whatever you sow, that is what you will reap.

Notes

1. Obadiah does not date his book directly, but various textual references suggest that his book dates back to the second half of the ninth century BC. An alternative date, which should be considered with caution dates the book to the fall of Jerusalem in 586 BC.
2. C.S. Lewis, *Mere Christianity* (New York: Macmillan, 1952).
3. www.yimpan.com/Songsite/lyric/index.asp?sid=3914
4. *The Sun*, 0/03/01
5. *Daily Star*, 31/10/01
6. *The Sun*, 18/02/02
7. http://oxfam.org.uk/campaign/cutconflict/asylum/asylumuk.htm
8. http://www.observer.co.uk/international/story/0,6903,610340,00.html – Martin Bright, "Fury as Zimbabweans sent to 'certain death'", 02/12/01

JONAH
(c. 760 BC)

≈≫ ⊱≪

Chapter 5

Re-commissioned for Service

"Racism is man's gravest threat to man –
the maximum of hatred for a minimum of reason."
(Abraham J. Heschel)

Jonah was swallowed by a big fish – fact or fiction? Many sophisticated and intellectual men and women have enjoyed ridiculing the authenticity of this Bible story. It's easy to be sceptical. "Would a big fish swallow a man whole? Could a man really survive for three days and three nights in its belly, as the Bible claims?" Attempting to answer the suspicions of sceptics, many liberal scholars, with weak and tenuous arguments, have argued that the story of Jonah is an allegory – a legend which was not intended to be understood as an historical account. Jesus Christ, however, speaking in a very matter-of-fact way, accepts the account as true: *"For as Jonah was three days and three nights in the belly of a huge fish, so shall the Son of Man be three days and nights in the heart of the earth"* (Matthew 12:40).

The book of Jonah is unique among the minor prophets. It has little prophecy contained within the message, for the story itself is the message. A very simple outline of the book is: Jonah disobeys; Jonah prays; Jonah obeys; and Jonah learns.[1] The book follows two main story lines: the story seen through the eyes of Jonah – "What's happening to me?" and the story seen through the eyes of the people Jonah encounters.

Firstly, "What's happening to me?" Jonah is represented as a strong-willed, fretful, pouting, hasty and patriotic man. God had called Jonah to be his voice to a foreign nation. He had instructed Jonah to go to Nineveh and preach against it, because its wickedness had come up before Him (1:1). Thus, Jonah was a man with a clearly defined mission – but Nineveh was no ordinary city. It was one of the great cities of the notoriously brutal Assyrian Empire. Israel well remembered Assyria's gross acts of violence. It was common policy among nations of this time period to build their empires by robbing other nations. The Assyrians were the most ferocious of them all. Their very name became a byword for cruelty and atrocity.

Probably on account of this, Jonah was disobedient: he renounced his mission. Instead of travelling to Nineveh to carry out his calling he ran away as fast as he could in the opposite direction. Did he run away because he was afraid? Did he lack confidence in his ability to carry out the task? No on both counts. When he finally arrived in Nineveh he demonstrated an ample ability to deliver God's message with both courage and confidence. The reason behind Jonah's disobedience was rooted in his understanding of God. He knew very well the merciful and compassionate nature of God. Therefore, he would not be complicit in the Assyrians avoiding retribution for their revolting behaviour.

Having been called by God, Jonah was faced with three options: stay at home in his village and allow the Ninevites to perish without warning; go to the people of Nineveh to tell them that they would be punished – knowing and fearing that God would show mercy on them if they repented from their wicked ways; or thirdly, run away from delivering God's message and hope that God's judgement would come quickly on the Assyrians. For Jonah there really was only one viable choice. He could not bear to see the Assyrians go unpunished. He could not face the prospect of further acts of cruelty being perpetrated against his beloved country. He passionately wanted to see the Assyrians paid back for their evil and wicked ways. He would have no part in a potential rescue and so he ran away. It is reassuring and instructive to find the failings of Jonah's character so publicly exposed for us to learn from his mistakes.

Jonah thought he knew better than God. This sounds familiar, doesn't it? We always think we know best, believing that our plans are so much better, safer, more exciting and fun. Herein lies the problem. We need to realise that God's plan is always the best plan. God, from His vantage-point high in the mountain range of holiness, in the great peaks of love, mercy, grace and compassion, sees the whole picture. He knows how to put a plan together that makes our deepest plans seem ridiculous by comparison.

Like Jonah, we cannot run away from God. God exists everywhere. Everywhere we lay our feet, sail our ships and further still, He is present. He exists in churches and cathedrals, governments and council meetings, crack houses and brothels. He is omnipresent. God, in His grace, breaks down the confines of our understanding and exposes our limitations, just as He brought a fierce storm to expose and unlock Jonah's limited grasp of His greatness.

If Jonah's motivation to turn tail and run from his mission is boiled down to its constituent elements, all we are left with is bigotry and racism. As a race of people, Jonah hated the Assyrians; man, woman and child he loathed them. He regarded his own theology and religious views as comprehensive and correct, and the beliefs and opinions of those who differed with him as being wicked and false. He was swift to judge them. His views were set and would not be altered. He would delight to see each and every Ninevite die a horrible death.

There are many situations in the world today of barbaric behaviour deserving the judgement of God. But God has mercy on whomever He chooses. Our job, as Christians, is to speak His message – the gospel – wherever, and to whomever, He sends us. It is not our job to make judgements as to whom should God show mercy.

In the midst of the fierce storm that seemed certain to bring disaster for all aboard the ship sailing to Tarshish, another facet of Jonah's character shines through – his honesty. Jonah accepted responsibility for the storm, and therefore his disobedience: he asked the sailors to throw him into the sea so that their lives could be saved. He was willing to face the terrifying prospect of a watery grave to save the lives of the ship's crew. What a surprise it must have been then, that instead of drowning, he was swallowed by a huge fish!

In the thoroughly horrible environment of the big fish's belly, Jonah remembers God and fervently prays to Him, expressing his repentance and gratitude for God's grace (2:1–9). In whatever situation we find ourselves, however unsettling or terrifying, however disobedient we may feel, we would be wise to echo Jonah's prayer and remember God's faithfulness: He protects us and always seeks the best for us.

Let's concentrate on one of the key verses from Jonah's prayer: *"Those who cling to worthless idols forfeit the grace that could be theirs"* (2:8). There are many different types of idolatry. In Jonah's time it would have included fetishism, the worship of nature and the worship of deceased ancestors. These forms of idolatry continue to pervade our societies, albeit in an evolved form: consumerism; new-age religions; our culture's obsession with celebrity; our willingness to worship at the shrine of scientific discovery; and an acceptance of the ancient religions of the world.

> "The greatness of God and the sinfulness of human beings are the two massive reasons why all religions do not lead to God ... Then there are the bourgeois religions, which feed the religious instincts of the leisured classes and cost their adherents nothing. Even Islam, despite its high view of God, does not offer the worshiper intimacy with God: 'Allah reveals his message. He never reveals himself.' Unlike other holy books the Bible does not record the story of human beings in search of God, but of God in search of human beings."[2]

This verse is filled with an overwhelming sense of tragedy: men and women who worship idols, whatever form they take, walk away and turn their back on their only hope for true love. A path of vulnerability is necessary for us to find and to receive this love. We cannot allow our need for God's grace to be substituted by anything else.

After three days and nights Jonah finally found himself on dry land, vomited out of the big fish. As he recovered from his ordeal, the word of the Lord came to him a second time. God instructed him to go to the city of Nineveh and proclaim His message (3:1–2). He had been re-commissioned. He had been given a second chance in spite of his clear and open disobedience. God never gave up on him. He never left Jonah and He will never leave us. Jonah's life took a dramatic downward turn as a result of his poor decisions, but God drew him back to do His will. If you feel the pain of past disobedience to God's instructions, make a decision now to co-operate with God. Let Him realign you to His will. Attitudes, beliefs and character traits may have to change as He re-commissions you, but do not permit past disobedience to prevent present obedience.

Jonah obeyed the call of God and preached to the Ninevites. The Ninevites turned from their evil ways and God showed mercy on them. It was exactly what Jonah had dreaded; anger bubbled up inside him. His uncompromising attitude and dislike of the people to whom he had preached sparked a fierce reaction, and he reminds God of the conversation they had had before he left home:

> "O Lord, is this not what I said when I was still at home? That is why I was so quick to flee to Tarshish. I knew that you are a gracious and compassionate God, slow to anger and rich in love, a God who relents from sending calamity. Now, O Lord take away my life, for it is better for me die than to live."   (4:1–3)

God responds by asking, "Have you any right to be angry?" God's questions deserve answering. What right did Jonah have to be angry? He himself was an unworthy recipient of the grace and love of God, as he confesses in his prayer to God (2:6). He had no right. He should have rejoiced: he was the instrument God chose to save the lives of more than six hundred thousand people.[3]

Instead, Jonah sat down in a sulk, attended to his temporal needs and waited to see what would happen to the city.

How does God deal with disobedient prophets and servants? God provided Jonah with a big fish to preserve him (1:17), a vine to protect him (4:6), a worm to perplex him (4:7) and a scorching wind to plague him (4:8). God is committed to teaching, correcting, rebuking and training His servants in righteousness.

The vine cost Jonah nothing, neither energy nor involvement. It was simply a testimony to God's grace. God used the vine to reveal to Jonah his distorted priorities – he had more emotional response for a withered vine than for all the inhabitants of Nineveh. God had created the people of Nineveh: He formed them, nourished them and watched over them. He loved them and wanted to reveal His love to them. Of course He was concerned about this great city. Like Jonah, we need to see the people living in the great cities of our world through God's eyes.

It's easy to be critical of Jonah's selfish and inappropriate reaction. We could find ourselves, like the illustration in the gospels, pointing at the speck of dust in another's eye whilst paying no attention to the plank in our own. Even in the Christian community, Jonah's response is far too common: we get angry with God when He takes a blessing from us or doesn't give us something we think we deserve.

How much of Western civilisation and Christian culture is self-obsessed? Provided our needs are met and our appetites are satisfied, who really cares about the needs of a dying world? We must never reason, whether from a religious basis or not, that some people are more valuable than others. We may think we have exorcised the demons of racism that reveal themselves in a holocaust or the policy of apartheid – but sadly Jonah's bigoted attitude is still alive in our world today. Ageism, sexism, racism and class-based elitism: our society has them all.

The brutal attacks on Rodney King in the US and Stephen Lawrence in the UK serve as painful reminders of the outworking of racism in our societies. But it extends beyond the sphere of those who perpetrate these awful atrocities: it festers in any elitist culture of exclusion. An illustration of how this expresses itself is the institutionalised racism identified in the Stephen Lawrence inquiry: "Unwitting racism can arise because of lack of understanding, ignorance or mistaken beliefs. It can arise from well-intentioned but patronising words or actions. It can arise from unfamiliarity with the behaviour or cultural traditions of people or families from minority ethnic communities ... It is important to state at once our conclusion that institutional racism ... exists in both the Metropolitan Police Service and in other Police Services and other institutions countrywide."[4]

The Christian community must be on guard against this kind of institutional elitism. We should not only have no part in this behaviour; we should actively speak out against it.

Whether in times of failure, disobedience, blessing or obedience we should be consistently asking ourselves questions. In addition to "Why is this happening?" we should ask, "What can I learn from what is happening?" God uses the circumstances of our lives as opportunities for growth and development. He knows best; if He asks us to do something, He will give us the ability and resources to accomplish the task. He doesn't sponsor "failed projects". We can fall into the pit like Jonah, but thank God we can be brought back, saved from the fate we deserve and given a second chance to bring glory to His name. God is committed to achieving His purposes in our lives, however difficult we may make it with inappropriate behaviour. It is reassuring and worthwhile to remember that God's plan embraces our shortcomings and is not frustrated by our failures.

Let's now consider the wider story as seen through the eyes of the people Jonah encountered. The first group Jonah met are the sailors he paid to take him to Tarshish. The storm threatened disaster as it pounded at the ship. The sailors panicked and threw their precious cargo overboard in a desperate and unsuccessful attempt to weather the storm. When Jonah's conviction took hold of him the sailors were faced with a very difficult decision: whether to throw Jonah into the sea to calm the storm, which they were sure would kill him, or to row back to land. Hard though they tried, they could not reach land, *"for the sea grew even wilder than before. Then they cried to the LORD, 'O LORD, please do not let us die for taking this man's life. Do not hold us accountable for killing an innocent man, for you, O LORD, have done as you pleased.' Then they took Jonah and threw him overboard, and the raging sea grew calm. At this the men greatly feared the LORD, and they offered a sacrifice to the LORD and made vows to him"* (1:13–16).

These sailors, probably pagan men deceived by false gods, displayed a remarkable respect for the sanctity of human life. It's a stark contrast to the reality of the world in which we live. Throughout most of the Western world abortion is accepted, and euthanasia and embryo research are cautiously welcomed. Yet life is so very precious. The Bible is clear in its view that life begins at conception (Psalm 139). There is a fundamental problem, however, even without the biblical witness: the playing safe argument. When is it safe to kill an embryo? If you're still not convinced ask yourself this question: "was the embryo in your mother's womb actually you?" The answer must be yes. One cannot say, "it wasn't at day one but it was at day fourteen."[5]

> "A human embryo is not a potential human being;
> it is a human being with potential."
> *The Christian Institute*

Having disposed of their cargo, the sailors would have had no reason to continue their journey to Tarshish and may have returned home to Joppa. They had an amazing "fisherman's tale" to tell – they had thrown a Hebrew overboard to escape the divine punishment of his God. Such an outlandish story would have travelled far and wide. Jonah would have become a household name.

The news of Jonah's return and miraculous survival, therefore, would cause widespread controversy. A man believed to have met with a watery grave survived in the belly of a huge fish, vomited out onto a Mediterranean beach; his skin and hair, we assume, bleached by the great fish's gastric juices. News of his great escape and strange appearance would travel ahead of him as he completed his long overland journey to Nineveh. It was all part of God's plan: Jonah's disobedience added weight to God's message. Jonah reached the outskirts of the city and began to proclaim: *"Forty more days and Nineveh will be overturned"* (3:4). It was an unwavering message with no hint of mercy which would hit the Ninevites right between the eyes. How would these proud, impetuous and cruel people respond?

The Ninevites believed God, they declared a holy fast and all of them, from the greatest to the least put on sackcloth, a symbol of mourning and repentance. When Jonah's message reached the palace, the king rose from his throne, took off his royal robes, and like the people of Nineveh, he covered himself with sackcloth. Then he issued a proclamation: *"By the decree of the king and his nobles: Do not let any man or beast, herd or flock, taste anything; do not let them eat or drink. But let man and beast be covered with sackcloth. Let everyone call urgently on God. Let them give up their evil ways and their violence. Who knows? God may yet relent and with compassion turn from his fierce anger so that we will not perish"* (3:7–9). It was an amazing response: an entire city came to repentance and received the mercy and grace of God. The Ninevites received a stay of execution.

It is the inner cities of the world, the modern "Ninevehs", where some of the greatest challenges lie for both government and people of good will – whatever their belief system. Cities are growing fast. The "pull" of economic opportunity and facilities in cities throughout the world and the "push" of famine, natural disasters, insufficient employment and education, poor health-care and public services are encouraging migration into urban areas. Urban growth poses severe challenges: serious social problems due to our inability to accommodate a rapidly expanding population. Perhaps our reticence to change further exacerbates this problem. Politicians and professionals working in these areas are beginning to accept that more of the same ideas and solutions, repeating the attempts of previous generations, will only serve to further increase our hopelessness and despair. Many are concluding that alongside serious government and community initiatives, commitment to a spiritual dimension must be re-introduced. The Christian community must be filled with a godly compassion for the lost opportunities and wasted potential of a generation. The gospel is good news; it begins inside a person offering a new sense of self-worth and purpose for living. The power of personal transformation can impact impossible situations. Most secular organisations have gradually withdrawn from the inner cities. The Church is still involved. Thankfully some governments are beginning to pay lip service to the valuable part faith communities can play. Much more is needed.

The people of Nineveh were confused. There was an alarming lack of moral truth. The city was a morass of selfish, impulsive behaviour. Our society is equally confused. Millions and millions of people inhabiting the great cities in our world are living without meaning, purpose and moral direction. One of the reasons vast numbers of people have been gathered together is so that God may use us, His servants, to effectively reveal His love for these city-dwellers – bringing meaning, purpose and acceptance to many lives. God chooses to use us to carry His presence into the developing and decaying cities of our nations.

The Ninevites responded immediately to Jonah's message. How would the Western world today respond to the preaching of Jonah? Would there be sudden interruptions for news bulletins in television and radio programmes? A media coup publicising and sensationalising the message? Who would listen? A man thought to be dead, swallowed by a big fish, carried his bleached body hundreds of miles to preach to a foreign city. How would you respond?

We have been given a much greater figure than Jonah to enlighten our dark world. The story of Jonah has one more inviting and challenging twist. A twist unravelled hundreds of years later and made clear by Jesus Christ. He used this story as a parable, a forerunner to the greatest story in all of human history: the birth, life, death, burial and resurrection of Jesus, the Son of God.

In answer to the demands of unbelievers for a miraculous sign to prove His divinity, Jesus said,

> *"A wicked and adulterous generation asks for a miraculous sign! But none will be given it except the sign of the prophet Jonah. For as Jonah was three days and three nights in the belly of a huge fish, so the Son of Man will be three days and three nights in the heart of the earth. The men of Nineveh will stand up at the judgement of this generation and condemn it; for they repented at the preaching of Jonah and now one greater than Jonah is here."*
> (Matthew 12:39–41)

How will our generation answer this charge? The Ninevites repented on hearing Jonah's message; but our cities and nations are reluctant to change.

We have one greater than Jonah to whom we must answer. Every man, woman and child must deal with these questions about Jesus: Why did He die? Why and how is He alive? One day He will require from each person an answer to the question: "What did you do with my love for you? A love that caused me to die in your place so that I could forgive you of your sin, and through my resurrection empower you to live." The people of Nineveh sought and received God's help and forgiveness – we must learn from them. They repented and changed their way of living – we must do the same.

Fifty years ago I experienced God's forgiveness. Although, I was only ten years of age, this experience has stayed with me throughout my life: I have peace with God through Jesus Christ. His salvation is the greatest gift on offer in the universe, paid for with the highest price imaginable and is freely available to everyone, including you.

Questions to consider

▶ Do you hold attitudes towards others that are offensive to God?

▶ Are you running away form doing God's will?

▶ Are you asking "Why is this happening?" or "What can I learn from what is happening?"

▶ Are you living a selfish life in a world of need?

▶ Are you allowing past disobedience to prevent present obedience?

▶ Do you need to respond to God's offer of a second chance?

Remember
God cares about lost people, hates racism and
wants your involvement in shaping a better world.

Notes
1. Campbell Morgan, *The Minor Prophets* (Grand Rapids: Revell).
2. *Joy*, September 2002, Issue no. 096, 'DIY Religion or Revelation?' by Michael Green, p. 36, from his book, *But Don't All Religions Lead to God?* (Sovereign World/IVP, 2002).
3. *"But Nineveh has more than a hundred and twenty thousand people who cannot tell their right hand from their left"* (4:11) indicates children of a young age, probably children under three or four years of age. Assuming that they were a fifth of the population of Nineveh, a total population of six hundred thousand people can be assumed.
4. *The Stephen Lawrence Inquiry*, Chapter 6, paragraphs 6.17 and 6.39 at www.archive.official-documents.co.uk/document/cm42/4262/sli-06.htm
5. The Christian Institute, www.christian.org.uk/briefingpapers/sanctityof life.htm

MICAH
(740–725 BC)

❦

Chapter 6
Morality Matters

"Honesty is the best policy"

The town crier stands in the city square. "Hear ye, hear ye," he calls. Some pay attention, others walk by. It has always been so. Likewise, Micah says, *"Hear, O peoples, all of you, listen, O earth, and all who are in it"* (1:2). Other contemporary voices add weight, especially those of Hosea and Amos. Will the people listen?

The prophet brings charges against the people of Samaria and Jerusalem. He testifies against them about the socio-economic conditions prevailing at the time: corruption of the rulers; dishonesty of the merchants; greed and covetousness of the land owners; evil plans and schemes of many; worldliness of the priests and prophets; oppression; witchcraft; and the widespread idolatry of the people of Israel.

It is a serious charge sheet. The people are called to answer the indictment as in a court of law. There are many solemn words that demand our attention, for the same charges can be made against this generation. Thankfully, however, the book is punctuated with hope: there is the possibility of a better day, when judgement is averted and the people are again blessed.

How would you prefer to leave the court? Declared innocent, I hope. We had better answer the charge and, if necessary, change.

There are three sections to Micah's message:

- Lodging the charges against Samaria and Jerusalem (chapters 1–2);

- Holding the leaders, rulers and prophets accountable (chapters 3–5);

- The Lord presents His case and explains His sentence (chapters 6–7).

Lodging the charges against Samaria and Jerusalem

Micah's first message prophesies Samaria's doom (1:6) and promises a terrible fate for her children: *"Shave your heads in mourning for the children in whom you delight; make yourselves as bald as vultures, for they will go from you into exile"* (1:16). His prediction was proved frighteningly accurate when in 722–721 BC, thousands of Israelites were taken captive, including many children. They never returned home. Jerusalem was conquered in 586 BC, but unlike her northern neighbour, the people of Judah were allowed to return home seventy years later.

Any prophet who delights to speak calamity has not understood the heart of God. A loving father will discipline a disobedient child, lamenting "this is hurting me more than it is you." God is a loving father. His attitude was demonstrated by Micah who publicly mourned the future captivity of Samaria and Jerusalem as he delivered God's message: *"Because of this I will weep and wail; I will go about barefoot and naked"* (1:8). Micah knew that God would bring judgement, and his heart was heavy with anticipation.

Justice is an essential part of God's character – where would we be without it? Following the bombing in Omagh, Ireland, a father who lost his twenty-one-year-old son explained the motivation for bringing a civil action against the alleged perpetrators: "This is not about money . . . We are not looking for revenge, but we are looking for justice and we want people held accountable for the terrible thing that was done to our loved ones."[1]

Micah uses his poetic gift, with his mastery of metaphor,

innuendo and satire, to describe the events and facts of his time. His skilful use of Hebrew wordplays enabled him to prophecy to many of the towns he served as a prophet, with added poignancy (1:10–16). Each pun either affirmed, contradicted, or expounded the meaning of the town's name. Micah would not allow the people to forget this message; it was too important!

But the prophet also cries out to modern man, warning of judgement. The charges he makes against Samaria and Jerusalem may be interpreted with contemporary questions; Where is your heart? What is the object of your affections? Does anything satisfy your deepest needs? Do you thirst for something more? Sadly, as in his day, many people live a shallow, self-indulgent and materialistic life, devoid of meaning and purpose. The words of Jesus challenge us: *"If anyone is thirsty, let him come to me and drink. Whoever believes in me, as the Scripture has said, streams of living water will flow from within him"* (John 7:37–38).

With his contemporaries Hosea and Amos, Micah warns against any preoccupation with leisure and pleasure. The calamitous cocktail of drink (2:11) and sex (1:7) are indirectly cited as a recipe for disaster. The recipe has not changed. Many people are still making fortunes, profiting from our pre-occupation with drink, drugs and sex. A multitude of men, women and children have had their lives damaged, some destroyed in the process. These wicked schemers devise iniquitous plans in an attempt to distort and reprogram our values and priorities. Micah warns these people sternly, promising them great depths of misery and sorrow: *"Woe to those who plan iniquity, to those who plot evil on their beds!"* (2:1).

Being more specific, our media must take some responsibility for propagating the hedonistic side of a leisure and pleasure pre-occupation. Too often it underlines the message "If it feels good, do it", which is one of the foundations of post-modern philosophy.

Television in particular drugs the masses with many irrelevant and flippant programmes. For example, the "reality" shows encourage millions of people to waste their own lives watching other people waste theirs.

> Americans watch an average of more than 4 hours of TV a day.[2]
>
> By the age of 65, the average American adult will have spent nearly 9 years of his or her life watching television.[3]

The American Academy of Paediatrics Committee on Public Education commented: "By the time adolescents graduate from high school, they will have spent 15,000 hours watching television, compared with 12,000 hours in the classroom ... The average American adolescent will view nearly 14,000 sexual references per year, yet only 165 of these references deal with birth control, self-control, abstinence, or the risk of pregnancy or sexually transmitted diseases."[4]

Whilst advertising, newspapers, films and magazines must take seriously their part in fuelling our permissive society, television's pervasive influence leaves it with a greater charge to answer. Alongside the good things it has done in opening a window on the world for multitudes, it has also played a very significant part in polluting society, with key providers profiting from lust and fantasy.

An Evangelical Alliance study on youth behaviour in the UK showed that Christian young people's sexual habits were not significantly different from others in their age group. Observe how the New Testament church penetrated its society with a new value system. We must ask whether the modern Church is ignorant of the extent to which contemporary culture has infiltrated its thinking and behaviour.

The long-running debate about whether violence on television has become violence in the classroom and on the street should be over. To quote Professor Jeffrey Johnson, the leader of a recent study that links television viewing to violence: "The evidence has gotten to the point where it's overwhelming."[5] Over the past forty years, 3,500 research studies on the effects of media violence have been conducted; only a tiny minority have failed to show a distinct correlation between watching violence on television and committing acts of real-life violence.[6]

By the age of 18, American children will have seen an average of more than 200,000 acts of violence, including 16,000 murders on TV.[7]

The huge benefit of quick communication and easy access to information provided by the Internet is matched by the terrifying simplicity with which anyone can access pornography and a seedy sexual underworld, with paedophilia as one of its vilest poisons. Evil men and women seek to profit from people's sexual cravings.

The US National Center for Missing and Exploited Children interviewed 1,501 young people aged between 10 and 17 who used the Internet regularly. One fifth of these had received a sexual approach over the Internet in the last year. "One in thirty received an aggressive sexual suggestion, including being asked to meet somewhere; called on the telephone; sent regular mail, money or gifts. One in four had an unwanted exposure to pictures of naked people or people having sex in the last year."[8]

The privacy of the Internet conceals paedophiles. Global child pornography rings are using the Internet to facilitate their sordid schemes, increasing the numbers of victims of abuse by creating a market for pornographic images and an efficient, private delivery system. The gravity of the threat is still underestimated.

When the child pornography ring "Wonderland" was broken in 2001, more than 100 men were arrested in 107 co-ordinated raids across three continents.[9] "UNICEF estimates that 90% of investigations into paedophilia involve the Internet, and the sheer numbers of images available in newsgroups and password-protected sites bears out investigation of the medium. When police around the world busted the Wonderland Club in a co-ordinated operation, they found 750,000 pornographic images featuring 1,236 individual children who had been victims of sexual abuse. Online child pornographers are not simply exchanging old material they find elsewhere: a US study found that between 36% and 37% of people who exchanged paedophilic material online were also directly abusing children."[10]

Under the guise of freedom of expression, the proliferators who plot this evil must be restrained. Decent people must insist on a better policing system for the World Wide Web, for its dangers go far beyond misused sex and violence.

Does any of this really matter? Is there a price to pay? The prophet says it does matter, and warns that there is a dreadful price to pay worked out in both the present and eternal judgements of God. Micah challenged the people of Israel to change their evil ways. They did not listen. They were dragged into slavery and exile, every part of their life disrupted. What lost opportunity. What wasted potential. Wise people learn from history.

Holding the leaders, rulers and prophets accountable

Micah opens his second message by exposing a dramatic disparity, contrasting the beauty of the mountain of the Lord's temple, the home of justice and righteousness, with the ugliness of the corrupt and discredited structures and leaders who governed and ruled Israel.

The prophet questions the leaders: *"Should you not know justice, you who hate good and love evil?"* (3:1–2). He condemned the prophets, declaring their disgrace for compromising the truth and leading the Israelites astray.

> *"Her leaders judge for a bribe, her priests teach for a price, and her prophets tell fortunes for money. Yet they lean upon the LORD and say, 'Is not the LORD among us? No disaster will come upon us.' Therefore because of you, Zion will be ploughed like a field, Jerusalem will become a heap of rubble, the temple hill a mound overgrown with thickets."* (3:11–12)

This proud, prosperous and influential city was devastated and ruined. We must heed the warning, for these "symptoms" are discernible in Western governments today.

Unrighteous politicians, prophets and pastors have infiltrated our ranks. People from every period of history have suffered injustice at the hands of the strong and powerful. Bribery and corruption is widespread.

Governments across the world in the 1990s, including Italy, Brazil, Pakistan and Zaire have fallen, partly because the people they governed would no longer tolerate their corrupt politicians. Bribery is also flourishing in the UK. "We live in a country in which the culture of bribery has taken deep root. It is practised by some of the most famous firms in the UK, and connived at quite cynically by Whitehall."[11]

Eliminating corruption not only promises great spiritual reward but is crucial for reaching the broader goal of effective, fair and efficient government for the benefit of all. But how can corruption be controlled, let alone eliminated? The message must be familiar by now: a return to honest values, and a refusal to co-operate with corruption, by individuals living out the gospel in genuine repentance and a loving relationship with God.

In 1999 Jonathan Aitken, a former UK cabinet minister, was jailed for perjury. He tells his story:

> "Not since the days of Oscar Wilde had any public figure suffered so much vilification and punishment for telling a lie in a libel case. My own Icarus-like fall from cabinet minister to convicted prisoner had left me with broken bones and battered spirits. The damage felt even worse than it was because most of the humbling took place in public. Yet this noisily enforced humiliation was probably a necessity, for it turned out to be such an effective antidote to the poison of pride ... I may not be the best judge of how much I have changed. All I can say with certainty is that my family, my children, my close friends and several observers all comment favourably on the changes which they perceive in me. I can, however, identify the areas where I think the process is taking place, for I describe them as inward change, outward change and upward change.
>
> Inward change starts with asking the simple question: Who am I? For me it was an essential self-interrogation after

falling from a mountain top of political power into a mine shaft of media opprobrium. That fall was so disorientating that for a time I did not know the answer to my own question ... In the end there was only one response to the question 'Who am I?' with which I could live. It was: 'I am a sinner who wants to repent.' This cry for help did not go unheard.

From the starting point of inward change, many outward changes manifested themselves, particularly in the field of human relationships. Within the family all sorts of new and enriching horizons opened up as I had more time and willingness to share my fears, frailties and insecurities. This led to renewed bondings, particularly with my children, who seemed to prefer a father who was vulnerable to a father who was powerful.

None of these inward or outward changes would have occurred had it not been for the most momentous change of all. This was what I call the upward change, the change in my relationship with God. Here I begin to tread on holy ground, for I am still too full of awe and wonder to be able to write clearly about what has happened. I am not even capable of saying when it happened, for I cannot point to a blinding flash of light on the road to Damascus, not to an instant moment of conversion. Yet somewhere along the painful road of the journey described in this book, after many months of prayer and listening, my eyes opened and I recognised that I had accepted Jesus Christ into my heart as my Lord and my God."[12]

As chapter 4 reaches the heart of its message, the sun breaks through the clouds to shine in all its glory, radiating warmth and encouragement. Micah sees a future when the worship of God in an established temple will draw people from all over the world. He describes a setting of peace and blessing where God's Word and law will be honoured, taught and obeyed. It is a time of amazing restoration: the lame, weak and grieving will find solace and encouragement; and although the prophecy includes the unpleasant reality of captivity, it promises a joyous return to prosperity and triumph (4:6–13).

The beginning of chapter 5 puts Bethlehem, a small and insignificant town, on the map for all time: *"But you, Bethlehem Ephrathah, though you are small among the clans of Judah, out of you will come from me one who will be ruler over Israel, whose origins are from old, from ancient times"* (5:2). These words determined the birthplace of the great messianic leader – Jesus.

That is now history, but we live in an exciting time, for the verses which follow are yet to be fulfilled, *"his greatness will reach to the ends of the earth. And he will be their peace"* (5:4–5). Jesus is the Prince of Peace. Peace means much more than the absence of war. Peace is "shalom", wholeness in every part of life, an ideal desperately sought by every generation.

The chapter concludes with an assurance that the Israelites will be delivered from their tormentors and future captors, the Assyrians. But deliverance would come at a price:

> *"I will destroy your horses from among you and demolish your chariots. I will destroy the cities of your land and tear down all your strongholds. I will destroy your witchcraft and you will no longer cast spells. I will destroy your carved images and your sacred stones from among you; you will no longer bow down to the work of your hands."*
>
> (5:12–13)

God hates idols. He is disgusted that His people should worship "things" with eyes that don't see and ears that don't hear. Many "self-made" men and women today misguidedly think their success is entirely of their own making, and so they forget God. By implication, they bow down to worship themselves. The Bible speaks clearly to these people, *"But remember the LORD your God, for it is he who gives you the ability to produce wealth"* (Deuteronomy 8:18).

God hates the practise of witchcraft, yet in the Western world there is a growing interest in the occult. Witchcraft is glamorised in books, television programmes and films, each promoting its beliefs, often targeting the young. Modern witchcraft is an ensnaring and seductive false religion from which we must protect our children.

The Lord presents His case and explains His sentence

In his final message, Micah challenged the Israelites' religious practices. Their faith had become formal: a mere mechanical exercise; a duty rather than a delight. He calls for an audit on their life and worship: *"How have I burdened you?"* He asks (6:2–3).

It remains a tough question. A rash and reckless response might be to blame God, accusing Him of causing pain, suffering and hardship. He anticipated the Israelites' selfish, short-sighted perception and interpretation of the circumstances. He reminded them of their history and His past kindness and blessing (6:4–5). God had saved, protected and blessed them. He had done nothing to warrant their religious hypocrisy.

How would you answer God's question? We too, would be wise to remember the kindness and goodness of God in our lives.

The society in Micah's day was strikingly deficient in integrity, as is ours today (6:10–13). The recent unmasking of some multi-national companies as dishonest and corrupt provides a picture of the Western world's deteriorating moral and spiritual order. It has become too acceptable to lie. Whether half-truth, or whole-lie, it makes no difference: a lie is a lie.

Our young people – the future generation – mirror the disturbing deterioration of the West's morality. Many students today are unable or unwilling to embrace an ethical way of living. According to a study conducted by Rutgers University in America, over 70 per cent of all university students admit to cheating at least once (typically plagiarism).[13]

Morality is not an abstract concept. It is not a meaningless ideal that has no value or purpose. Neither is morality subjective. It represents an absolute standard of right and wrong. Forget the tenets of existentialism, nihilism and postmodernism, for morality is reality. It may be hard at times to know where to draw the line, but that does not deny the truth that a line exists. Truth is truth, and remains fixed regardless of what we see, think, feel or have the ability to understand.

It is time for a moral revival. We must learn, teach and do what is right. The old test of "whatever works is right" may be pragmatic, but it is inadequate. We must follow a different pattern. God has not only written the book on morality, but He came to earth to live it out and requires us to do the same: *"He has shown you, O man, what is good. And what does the LORD require of you? To act justly and to love mercy and to walk humbly with your God"* (6:8). This is a powerful antidote to partiality and religiosity.

Men and women who act like predators, eager to lie, cheat and steal in pursuit of selfish gain, must heed Micah's words. For there is a high cost to such a way of life: *"You will eat but not be satisfied"* (6:14); *"You will plant but not harvest"* (6:15). God's predictions may seem to be temporarily avoided in a narrow materialistic context, but what about true wealth and well-being? Living at peace with God, yourself and others requires honesty and integrity.

> "An honest answer is like a kiss on the lips."
> *Proverbs 24:26*

A society where "Love your neighbour as yourself" is the accepted philosophy will be a caring, secure community. Persisting in self-centred and dishonest ways will eventually undermine the foundations of any group of people. Micah forecasts misery if we continue to follow a selfish belief system.

Throughout the world there is an army of caring, selfless people, living out the gospel, sometimes in hostile situations. The Christian family world-wide must not slacken in these endeavours; rather they must increase the pace. They provide the clearest picture of a living, caring Christ which the people of our world will ever see.

Micah next describes a state of confusion: *"The godly have been swept from the land; not one upright man remains"* (7:2). Society was in chaos; the judicial system was a joke; bribery undermined the law; bloodshed intimidated the people. The powerful dictated and conspired to get their own way. Even families distrusted each other (7:5–6).

Disaster loomed on the horizon for Samaria and Jerusalem, and now it looms for our cities and nations. God delights to show mercy, but cannot ignore our lack of repentance. The judge would like to pronounce us innocent, but we are required to change our selfish, sinful ways. Without this change, all our pleading and begging cannot change the verdict: Guilty.

Though the world was falling apart around him, Micah does not lose hope (7:7). In the face of calamity, he clearly believes that a time will come when righteousness will prevail: *"Though I have fallen, I will rise. Though I sit in darkness, the L*ORD *will be my light"* (7:8). It is a confident vision of the future, established on God's promises.

Micah concludes with these wonderful words: *"Who is a God like you, who pardons sin and forgives the transgression of the remnant of his inheritance? You do not stay angry for ever, but delight to show mercy"* (7:18). What an amazing God we have, who longs to forgive and help individuals and communities live purposeful, happy and successful lives.

Questions to consider

▶ Are you fulfilling what the Lord requires of you – to act justly, love mercy and walk humbly with your God?

▶ Are you trying to succeed in business by selling your soul?

▶ Are you endeavouring to live with integrity?

▶ Are you addicted to television or anything else?

► Are you serving others?

► Are you worshipping your success?

If you know you are trapped by any addiction,
please ask for help.

Remember
Morality matters and honesty is the best policy.

Notes

1. *The Guardian*, Saturday 27 July 2002, "After four years, justice closes in on Omagh bombers", p. 4.
2. Nielson Media Research, 2000, "2000 Report on Television" from www.tvturnoff.org
3. Idem.
4. American Academy of Paediatrics Committee on Public Education, 01/2001, "Sexuality, Contraception, and the Media" at www.asp.org/policy/re0038.html
5. BBC News, 29 March 2002, http://news.bbc.co.uk/1/hi/entertainment/tv_and_radio/1899533.stm
6. Michael Rich, American Academy of Paediatrics, "Statement before the Public Health Summit on Entertainment Violence", 26 July 2000 from www.tvturnoff.org
7. American Medical Association, 1996, "Physician Guide to Media Violence", from www.tvturnoff.org
8. National Center for Missing and Exploited Children (US), Crimes Against Children Research Center and Office of Juvenile Justice and Delinquency Prevention, 06/2000.
9. *The Guardian*, 11th January 2001, "Global child porn ring broken" by Nick Davies and Jeevan Vasagar.
10. *The Guardian*, 24th April 2002, "Casting the net for paedophiles", by Sarah Left.
11. *The Guardian*, David Leigh, 9 June 1999, "Corruption unbecoming".
12. Jonathan Aitken, *Pride and Perjury* (London: HarperCollins, 2000), pp. 358–361.
13. "College a cheating haven", *Parents of Teenagers*, Feb/Mar 1992, p. 5.

NAHUM
(660–650 BC)

꒰꒱ ꒰꒱

Chapter 7

God's Vengeance – Curse or Comfort

"Seek freedom and become captive to your desires.
Seek God and find your liberty."
(Frank Herbert [adapted])

Nineveh's history recorded a time when the whole community repented at the preaching of Jonah. But Jonah was dead, his message long forgotten. The city had returned to her old ruthless ways.

There was no reason for alarm. Nineveh was an impressive and imposing city, the crowning jewel of the Assyrian empire. A metropolis full of beautiful wide boulevards, large squares, parks and gardens, Nineveh was a civilised, sophisticated and secure place. Her fortified walls towered one hundred feet high and encircled the city. The labour of a multitude of foreign captives had built a seemingly impregnable city. Even her natural location, the junction of the Tigris and Khoser rivers, offered the city protection.

Conquests and victories flowed uninterrupted for a hundred years, enriching Nineveh with the spoil of twenty nations. The treasures of Babylon and Egypt were given a new home in the palaces and temples of Nineveh. Foreign merchants flocked into the city bringing with them an impressive array of valuable, luxury items from a long list of countries: gold and perfume from Southern Arabia; linen and glass-work from Egypt; cedar wood from Lebanon; and furs and iron from Asia Minor.[1] Immense wealth from the ends of the earth poured into the gates of this great city for her inhabitants to enjoy.

Despite the empire being built on cruelty and brutality, it enjoyed a rich cultural heritage. The library established by King Assur-bani-pal, the grandson of Sennacherib, which can be found, in part, in the British Museum today, is considered by many to form the most valuable of all the treasuries of literature of the ancient world; thousands of flat bricks or tablets which contain, it is believed, a record of the history, laws and religion of Assyria.[2]

Assyria's self-confidence was overflowing. News that her army had silenced the threat of uprising and trouble in the Southern reaches of her empire by destroying the Egyptian capital, Thebes,[3] added to her arrogance. Her position seemed unassailable. Who could challenge her might? It was no longer important that a strange visitor had prophesied their doom. Life was better than it had ever been before.

In 722 BC the people of Judah saw something that terrified them. They witnessed the destruction of their neighbour, the northern kingdom of Israel, and the barbaric transportation of thousands of Israelites into captivity. There would have been no prizes for guessing who was next on the Assyrian list! In the years that followed, Assyria destroyed many of Judah's cities and besieged Jerusalem in 701 BC. By the grace of God the Jews survived. But it was a hollow victory. The people of Judah were tormented by fear and anxiety. Their focus had strayed from God. The Assyrian Empire had won their attention.

Enter Nahum. God does not want His people to live in a place of intimidation, held captive by the threats of their tormentors. God is a liberator and has power to subdue all their enemies, however strong. Even Assyria!

Nahum, considered by many to be the poet laureate among the

minor prophets, brought a two-fold message: comfort for the remaining Jews living under Assyria's shadow in Judah; and vengeance, the irrevocable destruction of the Ninevites.

These seemingly unreconcilable threads are elegantly woven together by Nahum in the opening chapter of his prophecy: *"The* Lord *takes vengeance and is filled with wrath ... The* Lord *is slow to anger and great in power ... The* Lord *is good, a refuge in times of trouble. He cares for those who trust him"* (1:2, 3, 7).

Nahum prophesised, *"with an overwhelming flood he will make an end of Nineveh"* (1:8). It came to pass. It is worth considering just how accurate Nahum was in his description of quite how the city would be ruined.

In 612 BC the Babylonian army, united with an army of Medes, led a campaign that captured the Assyrian fortresses and strongholds in the empire's northern reaches. The Babylonian army made its way south and laid siege to Nineveh, but her walls were too strong for battering rams, so the Babylonians decided to starve the people out.[4] After a long siege, rain fell in such abundance that the waters of the Tigris and Khoser rivers inundated the city, destroying one of her walls and washing away her defences. The attacking army received free access to the city and duly ransacked Nineveh. She was laid waste as ruthlessly as her kings had once ravaged the surrounding lands. This proud and cruel capital was destroyed so completely that it passed out of history and came to be regarded as a biblical myth. For centuries travellers passed over her ruins without knowing that this once mighty city lay buried beneath their feet.[5] In 1845 her ruins were rediscovered and excavated by the British archaeologist Austen Layard, undermining the scepticism of many liberal Bible scholars.

How could the Ninevites forget the day they paid homage to God? Why did they turn back to their old ways? What happened to the king of Nineveh's public proclamation? Was it amended or repealed? Was it the generational change – a failure to effectively educate their children in the ways of God? Perhaps it was constitutional, a re-working of their society's laws to reflect their rapid rise to prosperity, power and apparent self-sufficiency. However it happened, the Ninevites regressed spiritually and their society degenerated.

Moral and spiritual deterioration has progressively plagued the fabric of our society. We re-write our history to reflect our decline. The faith of the founding fathers of America is an indispensable part of the country's history, yet "to read most philosophers and historians of the American polity today is to learn that America is an historical embodiment of secular philosophy".

"Religion has become subordinate to liberty."[6] The laws America's founding fathers laboured over to facilitate its development have been misapplied, amended and declared unconstitutional. The decision in June 2002 of the Ninth Circuit Court of Appeals to declare the pledge of allegiance unconstitutional, because it contains the phrase "under God", demonstrates the West's descent into darkness.

Dr James Dobson, the founder of the influential Christian group Focus on the Family, highlighted the irony of the court's decision. He contrasted it with the response of one hundred and fifty members of the House and Senate, on the Capitol steps following the September 11 attacks. They gathered to sing "God Bless America": "While we stood frightened, grieved and resolute to fight the evil that struck our nation, we clung to our country's foundational principles and banded together for better or worse. That this activist court saw fit to deny millions of school children the right to acknowledge God is unconscionable."[7] The secularisation of society highlighted by this case is evident throughout the Western world.

Today, freedom has been taken hostage by many governments, political bodies and pressure groups throughout the world. They misunderstand and misapply the true meaning of the word.

Misused freedom can result in bondage, the very opposite of what it stands for.

The freedom our world enjoys is not freedom at all, especially when viewed in the life of individuals. How can people be free when they are addicts? Multitudes are addicted to sex, drugs, alcohol, wealth, fame, power and much else. This list is not exclusive to those who are medically diagnosed with addiction; it applies to and includes all who allow their sinful desires to damage and rule their lives, to whatever degree. A society that endorses the "pleasure-at-all-cost-principle" is a society ensnared by addiction.

The philosopher Epictetus was right when he said: "Freedom is not procured by a full enjoyment of what is desired, but by controlling the desire." If we are addicted, that leaves us in a difficult position. How can *we* control the desire? Speaking to the Jews who had believed Him, Jesus said:

> *" 'If you hold to my teaching, you are really my disciples. Then you will know the truth, and the truth will set you free.' They answered him, 'We are Abraham's descendants and have never been slaves of anyone. How can you say that we shall be set free?' Jesus replied, 'I tell you the truth, everyone who sins is a slave to sin. Now a slave has no permanent place in the family, but a son belongs to it forever. So if the Son sets you free, you will be free indeed.' "* (John 8:31–36)

Two important situations remain in contemporary society against which this prophet speaks. The first is tyranny and the abuse of power; the second is the hope and heartache of the cities of our age.

If only brutal empires and nations, like the Assyrians, were confined to the texts of ancient history books. The generations that lived through the First and Second World Wars, by observation or involvement, will remember the dreadful spectre of Stalinist and Nazi brutality. Many nations were involved in the barbarism of this era, and share in the responsibility for the death of millions. More than half a century later, the world is still paying a high price for these wars. In the years that followed the Second World War, the world breathed again, only for despotic Communism to grip millions. Decades later, at the turn of the millennium, the sages and political wise men, inspired by the death of the Cold War and the end of communist oppression in Eastern Europe, marked by the fall of the Berlin Wall, predicted a time of peace and tranquillity in the world. If only *their* prophecies came true!

The historically overt and visible tyranny and abuse of power in the Western world has not disappeared; it has simply become more covert, disguised by a rhetoric of "looking after our own interests". Meanwhile, beyond the shores of Europe and America, other dictators strut the stage. Swaggering about brandishing weapons and money, they terrorise and bully. The representatives of brutality and the ambassadors of hate snuff out the candle of hope for millions of people throughout the world.

The book of Nahum reminds us that God is watching. From the beginning of time He has witnessed and recorded every act of cruelty. The destruction of Nineveh assures us that he will take action and that He will bring justice to every unjust situation, once and for all. Said another way, if any transgression is not brought under the blood of Christ, it will be paid for.

Nineveh's destruction was a complete end. There was no negotiation, arbitration or appeal. Every situation in our society, past, present and future, which stands in opposition to God, will eventually be utterly and irrevocably dealt with by Him. No one will have a complaint. There is no further court of appeal.

We, like the people of Judah, should rejoice: *"Look, there on the mountains, the feet of one who brings good news, who proclaims peace! Celebrate your festivals, O Judah, and fulfil your vows. No more will the wicked invade you; they will be completely destroyed"* (1:15). What a wonderful message of comfort.

It is hard to imagine that in cities many people remain lonely. People fight their way along the streets, many so preoccupied with their own lives that they fail to raise a smile or even make eye contact with a fellow traveller. It's a faceless society where independence is dominant. Vast numbers of people trust nobody. Many friendships and relationships are based on selfishness. Crime flourishes and hope dies. In this culture, many are driven to a life of self-sufficiency, persuaded not to rely on anyone. Many are too busy to develop genuine and sincere relationships. "What is in it for me? Getting from A to B is all that matters. The journey is irrelevant." The truth is, the journey is just as important as the destination, and we all need the help of other people.

What we see on the streets of our cities is confirmed in the Bible. It has been argued that "the city represents man's rebellion against God. Urban development, as depicted in Genesis, is the result of our declaration of independence and self-assertion. It is our attempt at achieving security and creative purpose. Yet all our human efforts turn out in the end to be self-defeating."[8] The same commentator identifies the early biblical cities of Nod (Genesis 4:9–17) and Babel (Genesis 11:1–9) as nowhere lands, places of non-arrival and non-communication. Add to this the violence represented by the city of Nineveh, and we are left with a very pessimistic view.

As Christians, however, our message should not be, "Leave the city." Rather, we must respond to the needs of urban society. We must present an authentic, God-centred, interdependent and relational community, committed to serving the needs of others. By fulfilling God's desires and plans for our church communities, we can play our part in healing the injury that city life has caused.

In carrying out this mission we would do well to balance the preceding comments with a more up-beat and optimistic analysis of the opportunities offered in cities. Cities are characterised by a high concentration of people; physical accessibility; the uniform culture of urban man; anonymity (which makes people more open to change than in close-knit rural and village communities); high mobility; and the impact and influence of mass media.[9] All of which mean that many people are within easy reach of the Christian message!

If our desire to transform the cities of the world is not already established, we should consider the words of the nineteenth-century evangelist, D.L. Moody, "If we reach the cities, we reach the nation. If we fail in the cities, they will become a cesspool which will infect the entire country."[10] This assessment is still true today. Have we, as Christians, failed to act on Moody's warning? Is the overwhelming and escalating evidence of social, moral and spiritual breakdown in towns and cities the legacy of past failures? Nineveh's neglect of her spiritual responsibility, and her overweening cruelty and selfishness, eventually cost her everything.

Understanding an angry and vengeful God can be difficult. How can a loving God behave in this way? Dr Thomas Constable, a distinguished Bible scholar, provides a clear and concise answer. "One aspect of the message of Nahum is what it says about God. Nahum teaches the reader that to believe in God's love is to be sure of His wrath. If God is never angry, He does not love. His anger grows out of His love. Can you look at sin, pride, oppression and cruelty and not be moved? Then you do not love … Do you not care that women are being abused and children neglected by fathers who are so selfish that they think only of their own pleasures? Then you are incapable of love. If God cannot burn with hatred, He is a God incapable of love. To believe in His love is to be sure of His wrath."[11]

Let us bid farewell to Nahum with an examination of God's comforting words to Judah. The Jews had suffered mercilessly at the hands of the Assyrians. They had been brutalised, tortured and killed. Many had been removed from their homeland and lived as exiles and slaves in the greater Euphrates valley. Their beloved city and its Temple had been destroyed. It was a great comfort to them that the time for the fulfilment of God's promises had arrived. The time for their joyful return to the

Promised Land and the destruction of their tyrannical enemies had come.

There is coming a final judgement and place where everyone will account for the way they have lived. Nonetheless, many issues are settled during our lifetime, for we reap what we sow. God deals with the wicked one way or another. My confidence in this is unshakeable: I believe that sooner or later God will right every wrong and fulfil every promise. Who do you trust? Where is your confidence?

Questions to consider

► Are you truly free?

► Have you forgotten God's past mercy and kindness?

► Does your fear and anxiety win your attention?

► Are you helping your children develop a moral and spiritual foundation for their lives?

► If you live in a city have you become self-absorbed?

Remember
God is not mocked. He is watching over His word to fulfil it.
You can rely on His justice and promises.

The servant of the Lord does not strive.

Notes
1. G. Maspero, "Ancient Egypt and Assyria", p. 271 from www.christiananswers.net/dictionary/nineveh.html
2. See Easton's Bible Dictionary online at http://www.biblenet.net/library/ eastonsDictionary and search for "Nineveh".
3. Nahum mentions the fall of the city of Thebes (3:8) and is likely therefore to have written after this date, but before it rose to power again in 654 BC to give meaning to his rhetorical question in 3:8.
4. www.crystalinks.com/nineveh.html
5. Dr Constable's notes at http://www.soniclight.com/constable/notes.htm

6. Michael Novak, *On Two Wings: Humble Faith and Common Sense at the American Founding* (San Francisco: Encounter Books, 2001), p. 5.

7. www.religioustolerance.org/nat_pled3.htm

8. Jacques Ellul, *The Meaning of the City* (Eerdmans, 1971) in Eddie Gibbs, "Urban Church Growth", Grove Booklet on Ministry and Worship No. 55 (1977), p. 11.

9. Donald McGavran, *Bridges of God*, in Eddie Gibbs, "Urban Church Growth", Grove Booklet on Ministry and Worship No. 55 (1977), p. 11.

10. www.urbanleaders.org/Urban_Leadership/Urban_Leadership_Case_Study_1200.htm

11. Dr Constable's notes at http://www.soniclight.com/constable/notes.htm

HABAKKUK
(c. 600 BC)

❧ ❧

Chapter 8
Faith Answers Questions

"In faith there is enough light for those who want to believe and enough shadows to blind those who don't."
(Blaise Pascal)

The book of Habakkuk begins with a wail of despair and closes with a shout of confidence. The key to this startling transformation is a secret worth treasuring. When circumstances in life leave us crying out "Why, God?" this prophet is a welcome companion. Habakkuk identifies with our frustrations as we try to understand why good people suffer.

The curtain rises on Habakkuk's prophecy, revealing a man tormented by the abhorrent unfairness that surrounded him. "Why, God?" he pleads at the sight of crookedness. A hundred different manifestations of evil confronted him. He saw people who trusted in God suffering oppression and persecution at the hands of proud and brutal people.

Why was there no justice? He saw people profiting from evil, liars and cheats being rewarded with strength and power, while those who were righteous became weaker. If the injustice in his own nation wasn't enough to confound him, the rising power of the ruthless Babylonians was more than sufficient. He saw this puffed up and impetuous nation rise to power, and begin to dominate Middle Eastern politics. He saw the Babylonians rape and pillage the northern cities of Judah and relentlessly advance against Jerusalem, his nation's capital. The people of Judah

appeared to be destined for death and extinction. Most disturb-
ingly of all, God appeared inactive.[1]

The immorality and injustice in the kingdom of Judah was too
much for Habakkuk to bear. "Why don't you do something,
God?" he cried. *"How long, O LORD must I call for help, but you do
not listen? Or cry to you, 'Violence!' but you do not save? Why do you
make me look at injustice? Why do you tolerate wrong?"* (1:2–3).
Habakkuk wrestled to reconcile and understand what he saw
with what he believed.

God's answer amazed Habakkuk. He would use the cruel and
violent Babylonians to deal with the rampant injustice in
Habakkuk's home nation (1:6–7). In graphic and poetic language God describes the Babylonians' military advance (1:8–11).

This response was deeply disturbing. How could a holy God
use wicked people to bring justice? Habakkuk questioned God
again: *"Why are you silent while the wicked swallow up those more
righteous than themselves?"* (1:12–13)

With unambiguous clarity God revealed that He had seen all
and would judge all. He would use the wicked Babylonians to
punish Israel, but the Babylonians would pay dearly for their
crimes. This puffed-up nation, God explained, would taste His
wrath. Their greed would lead them to an early grave (2:5). They
would pay for piling up stolen goods and gaining wealth by
extortion (2:6). Injustice would not prevail. Those who plot the
ruin of other people would be held accountable. God would
bring judgement. The Babylonians would reap what they had
sown (2:7). God promised an overwhelming wave of justice
which would devastate the Babylonians.

As Habakkuk grappled with his concerns, God revealed a
philosophy of life that would answer Habakkuk's questions. A
way of life beautiful in its simplicity and rich in its reward. *"The
righteous will live by his faith"* (2:4). This is the key to Habakkuk's
transformation; this is the secret worth treasuring. One commentator writes, "This verse is similar to the constricted part of
an hour-glass. Everything that precedes it leads up to it, and
everything that follows results from it. It is like a doorway
through which everything in the book passes."[2]

Faith did more than just satisfy Habakkuk's appetite for answers. It transformed him. Saturated with confidence, he speaks a hymn of praise and prayer to God: *"L*ORD*, I have heard of your fame; I stand in awe of your deeds, O L*ORD*. Renew them in our day, in our time make them known"* (3:2). Habakkuk sang of God's greatness, His awesome and supreme justice: *"His glory covered the heavens and his praise filled the earth"* (3:3). He remembers God's past acts of judgement (3:12–14). Habakkuk had a revelation, a terrifying vision of justice in action. His legs turned to jelly at the thought of God bringing justice (3:16). He was awestruck. His new-found understanding of God's justice brought an important qualification to his initial cry for judgement – *"in wrath remember mercy"* (3:2).

Transformed from wavering uncertainty and confusion to clarity and confidence, Habakkuk brings the curtain down on his prophecy with a statement capturing his new philosophy of life: *"This is how I shall live from now on,"* he says, *"Though the fig-tree does not bud and there are no grapes on the vines, though the olive crop fails and the fields produce no food, though there are no cattle in the stalls, yet I will rejoice in the L*ORD*, I will be joyful in God my Saviour"* (3:17–18).

If Habakkuk did not believe in an all-powerful, all-knowing God there would have been no point to his cries for justice. To whom could he complain? The truth is that without God there would have been no basis to his complaints. If you refuse to believe in God, you're wasting your breath when you keep asking, "Why?" If you believe that there is no supreme, all-powerful and all-knowing God in control, to whom can you appeal for justice? The outworking of this philosophy is a world where man is left to fight for his own survival. This worldview offers one hope – the righteousness of mankind – which history teaches us as holding no hope at all. The first lesson of Habakkuk is that if you don't believe in a righteous and sovereign God, you have no reason to complain!

"Standing with my boots knee deep in the reeking muck of a Rwandan mass grave where thousands of innocent people have been horribly slaughtered, I have no words, no meaning, no life, no hope if there is not a God of history and time who is absolutely outraged, absolutely burning with anger toward those who took it into their own hands to commit such acts."[3]

What method should we adopt for answering the difficult questions of life? Martin Lloyd-Jones outlines the ground rules which Habakkuk used to silence his wail of despair:[4]

1. To think instead of speaking.
2. When you start thinking, you must not begin with your immediate problem, but begin further back.
3. Put the particular problem in the context of those firm principles which are before you.
4. If you are still not clear about the answer, then take it to God in prayer and leave it with Him.

This action involves the deceptively simple truth: God will be your God. "The covenant promise that God will be your God is spectacular beyond imagination. It means that God engages all His omnipotence and all His omniscience all the time to do good to you in all the circumstances of your life with all His heart and all His soul."[5] God says, *"They will be my people, and I will be their God ... I will never stop doing good to them ... I will rejoice in doing them good ... with all my heart and soul"* (Jeremiah 32:38–41).

Having given the problem to God, we must consciously leave our concerns, worries and frustrations with God. We expect God to answer (2:1), and watch and wait with patience. When He speaks we write down the answer (2:2).

"Though the mills of God grind slowly, yet they grind exceeding small; though with patience he stands waiting, with exactness grinds he all."
Friedrich von Logue

Although sometimes it appears to us as if God is acting slowly, He isn't. God is always exactly on time. He deals with all situations with tremendous accuracy and without delay. When facing injustice in the world, remember God's answer to Habakkuk: *"For the revelation awaits an appointed time; it speaks of the end and will not prove false. Though it linger, wait for it; it will certainly come and will not delay"* (2:3).

God told Habakkuk to record the prophecy. What a tragedy it would have been if he had failed to obey. His revelation, and the powerful and encouraging lessons it teaches us, would have been lost forever. Furthermore, the strength of the challenge to his own generation would have been weakened.

As God speaks to you, follow Habakkuk's example. The words may not endure for thousands of years, but they may provide direction and encouragement in your life, confirm what God has otherwise spoken, and act as a reminder of God's unfailing promises.

Faith was the answer to Habakkuk's perplexity. Faith empowered him to climb out of the depths of despair to deliver a passionate declaration of his confidence in the sovereignty of God. But what is faith? What does it mean that *"The righteous will live by his faith"* (2:4)?

True faith is more than a confident belief. The New Testament teaches us that *"Faith is being sure of what we hope for and certain of what we do not see"* (Hebrews 11:1). The Christian faith is not blind faith. On the contrary, it has a reasonable basis.

Habakkuk did not simply shut his eyes to the injustice that surrounded him – he endured it – because his faith enabled him to trust in God's plan for justice. This is a common misconception among non-Christians, as expressed by the philosopher Friedrich Nietzche, who asserted, " 'Faith' means not wanting to know what is true." This position may be easily rebutted by recognising the truth that "My heart cannot rejoice in what my mind rejects."[6]

Habakkuk's leap of faith came from understanding that God is eternal, holy, almighty and faithful. He reasoned from what he knew and was therefore confident of what would happen. Habakkuk realised that there was no need to be confounded by the injustice that surrounded him. He had a revelation that gave root to a deep conviction that God was in control.

> "Faith is to believe what you do not see;
> the reward of this faith is to see what you believe."
> *Augustine*

When we reach an impasse in our understanding, we, like Habakkuk, must be courageous and confess who God is and what He has done for us.

A life of faith is not achieved in a day. Learning to trust in God no matter what comes our way, takes time to develop. Without faith, the New Testament declares, *"it is impossible to please God"* (Hebrews 11:6). If pleasing God is important to you, then building a life of faith, trust and confidence in God should be a priority. The life of faith is a developing journey. If you have stumbled or fallen over, rise up and start walking again. Habakkuk reached a new place of confidence and trust in God. So can you. It is worth the effort.

Some food for our journey

In the early days of Jesus' ministry His disciples asked Him to teach them how to pray. These men were young Jews who knew the Old Testament. They knew God as Jehovah: the great deliverer; the all-powerful one. Their theology emphasised God's covenant relationship to the nation as a whole, but not God as Father to each of them. They considered God to be so holy that they would not even say His name!

Answering their question, Jesus told them to begin their prayers with "Abba". To address God as "Daddy". They were shocked. This was a radical revelation: "Call Jehovah Daddy?!"

The all-powerful, all-knowing covenant God could be addressed as father! This was an unparalleled level of intimacy, indicating a relationship of love and trust with God, the perfect Father; a relationship that defined them as "children of God" and had the potential to destroy all their insecurity.

Like babies, growing and developing without fear or anxiety, secure in our parents' love and care, we too can trust our lives into the hands of our heavenly Father. In Him we have found someone who will never fail or desert us; someone we can truly trust. We can have faith in such a God.

When Habakkuk came to a new understanding of the greatness of God, it changed him. His wail of despair became a shout of confidence. He had faith to trust his life and the affairs of his nation into God's hands. Habakkuk teaches us that faith answers questions.

Questions to consider

▶ Do you have faith in God?

▶ Are you still angry with God about some past experience?

▶ When you pray, do you leave your anxieties with God?

▶ Do you write down what you believe God has spoken to you?

▶ Is it time to review what you wrote down some time ago?

Remember
Without faith it is impossible to please God.

Notes

1. Adapted from *Dr Constable's Notes on Habakkuk*, 2002 edition, p. 5 at http://www.soniclight.com/constable/notes.htm
2. *Dr Constable's Notes on Habakkuk*, 2002 edition, p. 4 at http://www.soniclight.com/constable/notes.htm

3. Gary Haugen, *Good News About Injustice* (Leicester: InterVarsity Press, 1999), p. 85.
4. Lloyd-Jones, *From Fear to Faith* (London: InterVarsity Press, 1972), pp. 25–41.
5. John Piper, *God's Covenant with Abraham*, 4 December 1983, Bethlehem Baptist church at http://www.soundofgrace.com/piper83/120483m.htm
6. Josh McDowell, *Evidence That Demands A Verdict* (San Bernadino, CA: Here's Life Publishers, Inc., 1988), pp. 3–4.

❧❧ ❧❧

Chapter 9

What You Believe Matters

*"Superstition, idolatry and hypocrisy have ample wages,
but truth goes a-begging."*
(Martin Luther)

I remember as a young boy watching the soccer cup final on a tiny home-made TV. There was a limited choice in broadcast channels and programmes, but all showed a high regard for good taste. My grandchildren have a different experience: digital and interactive, on plasma screens with programmes about everything, and good taste no longer seems to be regarded as important.

In my childhood, horoscopes belonged in almanacs. Now they are everywhere. Most places of worship were churches. Now there are temples to every god in all our major cities and towns. The world has become a global village for the wealthy, first world inhabitant. In this global village, food, entertainment, culture and travel are enjoyed in abundance.

One more reminiscence from childhood: at New Year, the person with the darkest hair carried a piece of coal across the threshold of many houses to bring good luck. This and many other strange superstitions continue. There are so many options and choices for spending time and money, all part of the dilemma of the digital age.

Why make these observations? Nobody seems to be getting hurt. People can practise and believe what they want; surely it's nobody's business? Does it matter? Is it important? Is there a price to be paid for our behaviour? The ancient prophet Zephaniah has a view: he believes it is very important.

Zephaniah was a contemporary of the prophets Nahum, Habakkuk and Jeremiah. In the same way that God had sent Jonah, Amos and Hosea to deliver a series of final warnings to wayward Israel, He appointed these men to deliver a forceful eleventh hour warning to Judah. Judah had slipped into a pitiful spiritual state since the death of King Hezekiah in 686 BC. Hezekiah's successor was Manasseh, whose reign was as long as it was wicked (686–642 BC). Political expediency permitted foreign ambassadors to set up shrines and temples to their gods. Political dissenters and those choosing to live a righteous life-style were not tolerated.

Despite king Manasseh's repentance late in life and his attempts to draw Judah back to serve the Lord their God, idolatry was firmly established. After his death in 642 BC, his son Amon took the throne, turning his back on his father's late reforms. In his short reign, the nation reverted to wicked practices. When Josiah ascended the throne in 640 BC, as an eight-year-old boy, the nation of Judah was in a sorry condition. Pagan cults and practices both native and foreign were flourishing. The apparatus of fertility religions and the ritual of sacred prostitution were being practised even within the Temple of the Lord. Divination and magic, which enjoyed enormous popularity in Assyria, were the vogue in Jerusalem, as were foreign fashions of various sorts (1:8). The barbarous rite of human sacrifice made its appearance again.[1]

Zephaniah spoke out against these vile practices. Blessed with royal blood (he was the great grandson of King Hezekiah), he almost certainly had access to the royal courts. He was probably among a group of advisors and counsellors who supported and inspired King Josiah. The young king removed the idols and purified the practice of the Jewish faith.

Zephaniah's prophecy, in a similar vein to Nahum, can be divided into good and bad news. The effect of the news you receive is dependent on your attitude to God. Sometimes bad news can alter its face and smile instead of scowl. The key to the transformation, which Zephaniah endorsed, is genuine repentance. He prophesied that God would catastrophically intervene to judge humanity's wickedness, its idolatry, superstitions, pluralism, syncretism, indifference and complacency. God promised that for those who repented, He would restore the conditions He originally intended them to enjoy.

Zephaniah spoke specifically about idolatry, especially Baal worship; astrology; people who swear by Molech; people who turn their back from following the Lord and superstition.

Idolatry

"I will cut off from this place every remnant of Baal, the names of the pagan and idolatrous priests" (1:4). The influx of gods from other cultures had contaminated the Jewish faith. Baal, the principle male god of the Phoenicians was fervently entreated for the protection of livestock and crops. The "advantages" that another god appeared to offer were irresistible for many. The proletariat were seduced to worship this weather-god, because their prosperity depended on the productivity of the crops and the livestock of the landowners, whose land they worked.

The religious ceremonies associated with Baal worship were an unpleasant ordeal. They included burning incense and offering burnt sacrifices, occasionally involving human victims. The officiating priests would dance around the altars, frantically chanting and cutting themselves with swords and spears to inspire the attention and compassion of Baal (1 Kings 18:27). Baal's female counterpart, Asherah, the goddess of fertility, equally depraved her worshippers by encouraging the practice of temple prostitution. God was angry that the people of Judah had chosen to worship these false gods, and moved, as on previous occasions, to rid the nation of the priests and leaders who encouraged such worship.

Western society's obsession with sex and sensual lust, along with the rise in paganism, shamanism and druidism, serve to illustrate some modern manifestations of Baal and Asherah worship.

Astrology

"I will cut off ... those who bow down on the roofs to worship the starry host" (1:5). The twentieth century witnessed an amazing awakening of interest in star-signs, horoscopes and all things associated with the zodiac. Almost every newspaper and "life-style" magazine has a section devoted to astrology. In an age of science and reason, it is staggering that many educated people, having turned their backs on Christianity, are openly accepting different and dangerous alternatives.

Syncretism and pluralism

"I will cut off ... those who bow and swear by the LORD *who also swear by Molech"* (1:5). The people of Judah were not willing to put all their trust in Jehovah; they wanted to spread the risk by seeking all apparent blessings from every available god. These people worshipped God and spoke out their loyalty to Him, but they also followed the vile god Molech. Just as most humans hate even the idea of being "two-timed", God hates and refuses to tolerate syncretism, the adulteration of true worship with other religions. Practitioners of this philosophy will be judged for their dreadful disloyalty to God.

Molech was the national god of the Ammonites, a ferocious and demanding deity to whom children were sacrificed by fire to please and appease him. God so hated the practice of child sacrifice that He provided a specific and definitive law to abolish it: *"Do not give any of your children to be sacrificed to Molech, for you must not profane the name of your God. I am the* LORD*"* (Leviticus 18:21).

When we compare God and Molech, it's hard to imagine how anyone would choose Molech. But that is exactly what the Jews did! One encourages its believers to sacrifice the precious life of a child; the other promises to help parents raise their children to reach their potential and achieve greatness. One god involves its adherents in lewd and degrading behaviour; the other offers to help them live out the true nobility of their humanity. One consumes precious children with fire (2 Kings 23:10); the other confirms His power and greatness by protecting his followers with fire (Exodus 13:21). Need I go on?

What a tragedy that Molech worship is still with us today. As Melvin Rhodes writes:

> "Although almost 14 years have passed, the picture remains a vivid memory in my mind. A policeman stands outside a courtroom holding in his left hand the head of a 6-year-old boy, decapitated in a ritualistic child sacrifice. The gruesome murder took place in West Africa. The perpetrators of the heinous act, including at least one close relative of the boy, were caught, tried and executed within a few weeks. But the reality of child sacrifice continues to this day ... Two months after the decapitation mentioned above, Libyan terrorists blew up a Pan Am airliner over the Scottish town of Lockerbie, killing 270 people, including several children. A picture in one of the newsmagazines showed a young girl who had died on the plane. Someone who had met her at the airport before the fatal flight left flowers for her, accompanied by the simple inscription: 'Little girl, you didn't deserve this.'
>
> ... I remember expressing my horror at this appalling terrorist act, voicing my contempt for the inhumanity of anyone who could so easily blow up hundreds of blameless people, including innocent children. But one person's response shocked me – and reverberates to this day: 'You Americans make such a fuss about the loss of a few children killed by terrorists. Yet you murder millions of your own children every year.' He was talking about America's child sacrifice: abortion."[2]

In the name of choice, millions of children are sacrificed – conceived but never born. No "choice" is offered to the babies, knitted together by God in a mother's womb for rich and fulfilling lives (Psalm 139). The untold loss to the pool of human resource, genius and creativity is too awful to contemplate. I am confident that if William Wilberforce were alive today, he would campaign as vigorously against the moral iniquity of abortion as he did against slavery.

The parallels between child sacrifice and abortion are many, most notably – the sober fact which cannot be denied – parents kill their own offspring, whether as a sacred rite or with the excuse of "choice". Can any society that endorses parents killing their children call itself civilised?

> In developed countries, **every minute** there are 26 unplanned pregnancies and 18 abortions.[3]

Molech worship, however, is more widespread than abortion. The *Oxford Illustrated Dictionary* defines the name as a "power or influence to which everything is sacrificed". People today sacrifice health, relationships and family life, destroying children, marriages and their bodies in an obsessive quest for power, fame, influence and sexual satisfaction. Molech is again asking for excessive sacrifice. Those who continue to "swear by Molech" God declares, will be "cut off" from the face of the earth.

Pluralism is the adoption of the stance, "all roads lead to God" (with the caveat, "if God exists ..."). It may seem an unavoidable reality in the world of the twenty-first century. In our age, you are free to believe in whatever god you prefer, to pick and choose, to mix and match whatever combination of gods suit your lifestyle and personality. To this position Zephaniah issues a warning. The step from recognising plurality to embracing pluralism is a step too far for the biblical prophets.

> "Pluralism argues that each position (even opposing positions) must be accepted as equally true and valid ... Pluralism is not a statement on whether a view should be allowed a valid opportunity to present its perspectives. Rather, it is an epistemological commitment that no truth claims, moral or otherwise, can be said to be more true or valid than others."[4]

The biblical prophets resolutely maintain their dogmatic and apparently intolerant position, arguing that there is but one

God, and that all other gods are false. Christian belief mirrors the prophets, for Jesus said, *"I am the way and the truth and the life. No-one comes to the Father except through me"* (John 14:6). Christianity cannot be reconciled with other religions without being re-written. It is exclusive because of its claim to truth. To argue that all religions are essentially the same is to misunderstand their different claims.

Adopting the "all roads lead to God" position runs in total contradiction to Christianity and effectively makes its believers the founders of their own religion. In the Buddhist religion there is reputed to be no god, whereas Hindus' claim three hundred and thirty-three million gods. These differences are irreconcilable. Zephaniah makes it clear that the overlapping practices of idolatry, syncretism and pluralism will be dealt with harshly.

To Zephaniah's warning, I add my own. The exclusive claims of the Christian faith are not an excuse to impose Christianity on any people. On the contrary, every human being is allowed to worship whoever and whatever they choose – a right endorsed in international law. If only religious freedom was strictly upheld, at least in every country that has signed up to such agreements. Sadly today, many Christians are martyred and persecuted for their faith. Moslems, Buddhists, Jews and Hindus also suffer persecution, even death. None of this behaviour is acceptable.

Turning away from god

As chapter 1 unfolds, Zephaniah addresses a more subtle sin. It is neither public nor degrading, but is nonetheless important and equally destructive. He condemns *"those who turn back from following the LORD and neither seek the LORD nor enquire of him"* (1:6). The judgement is earned by individuals relying on their own judgement and failing to enquire of Him. This lack of spiritual discipline causes people to turn back, to forget the Lord and follow their own way. In the words of Isaiah, *"We all, like sheep, have gone astray, each of us has turned to his own way . . ."* (Isaiah 53:6). This is pride. Millions of people in the Christian world fall into this category. In the near or distant past they have had a relationship with God, and worshipped with other Christians. The pressures of life, a misunderstanding, some disappointment or just plain carelessness find them not seeking the Lord. If these words strike a chord with you, please return to the Lord and find fellowship with other Christians. Whatever the cost in humbling yourself or reprioritising your life, I urge you to act. The prophet's warning requires action and repentance.

Superstition

"I will punish all who avoid stepping on the threshold" (1:9). The historic root of this practice is found in a story from the time of Samuel, a prophet five hundred years or so before Zephaniah. The ark of God was captured by the Philistines, and placed in the temple of Dagon, one of their gods. *"When the people of Ashdod rose the next day, there was Dagon, fallen on his face on the ground before the ark of the LORD!"* (1 Samuel 5:3). The Philistines took Dagon and propped him up, back in his usual place.

> *"But the following morning when they rose, there was Dagon, fallen on his face on the ground before the ark of the LORD! His head and hands had been broken off and were lying on the threshold; only his body remained. That is why to this day neither the priests of Dagon nor any others who enter Dagon's temple at Ashdod step on the threshold."*   (1 Samuel 5:45)

So a superstitious tradition began which was handed down from generation to generation.

Superstition conceals itself with many masks, sometimes in bizarre activity, like stepping over the threshold. At other times it appears to include a sensible rationale, such as not walking under ladders. Touching wood and wearing or carrying lucky charms have no logic whatsoever. Ezekiel wrote, *"Therefore this is what the Sovereign LORD says; 'I am against your magic charms with which you ensnare people like birds, and I will tear them from your arms'"* (Ezekiel 13:20). He concludes that superstition is dangerous because it traps people.

Superstition reaches deep into our society. The expression, "touch wood" is used as a protection from failure and misfortune. This widespread practice is thought to originate from pagan times when trees were held in high esteem and were believed to be inhabited by "wood spirits". To touch a tree with respect indicated that a person was seeking protection from a particular wood spirit.

If you break a mirror, do you fear seven years of bad luck? This superstition originates from an old idea that a person's soul is present in their reflection, and by smashing a mirror, your soul is damaged, bringing bad luck or early death.

For the Chinese and Japanese Americans, the fear of the number four can be a real killer. "On the fourth of each month", an American journalist writes, "cardiac deaths for Chinese and Japanese Americans spike 7 percent compared to others days, according to a massive new study by a team of scientists at the University of California-La Jolla."[5] Why? The cause of the rise is believed to be due to increased stress and anxiety levels as a result of a superstition. In the Japanese and Chinese languages, the number four sounds like the word for death. "It's considered so unlucky in China and Japan that many hospitals don't list a fourth floor, the Chinese airforce avoids assigning the number four to its planes, and the 'Simpsons' cartoon show was initially a flop in both countries – because Homer and Bart and the other characters only have four fingers."[6]

Superstition is widespread. It is reported that Michael Jordan, the basketball superstar wore his "lucky" college gym shorts under his Chicago Bulls uniform throughout his entire NBA career. It is also said that golf sensation Tiger Woods usually wears red on Sunday because he believes it is a "lucky" colour. Even presidents have fallen for the seductive charm of superstitions. It is believed that President Roosevelt, who travelled continually, would never travel on a Friday.

Many people are ruled and regulated by the practice of superstitious beliefs. Why should they be dominated and controlled by irrational fears? Under a pretence of safety and comfort, superstitions bind people to habits and patterns of thought that limit the development of their full humanity. This is not freedom, but bondage.

Zephaniah's warnings form a catalogue of indictments against God's people. The prophet warns us that, *"The great day of the Lord is near – near and coming quickly ... That day will be a day of wrath, a day of distress and anguish, a day of trouble and ruin, a day of darkness and gloom"* (1:14–15). On this day the blood of the people who have sinned against the Lord will be poured out like dust, *"neither their silver nor their gold will be able to save them"* (1:18).

The phrase, *"The day of the Lord"* has a variety of interpretations, sometimes referring to the past, the near future and sometimes the distant future. The phrase is generally considered to refer to a period of time when God is working in a recognisable way. Whether it is a time of blessing or judgement is dependent on our and our nation's attitudes to God.

So what of today? Whether we are naïve, ignorant, deceived or deliberately disobedient we will, sooner or later, be asked to pay the price for behaviour that reflects the actions described by Zephaniah. What happened to the "sinners" of their day will happen to those who persist in following the practices of these ancient people. The warning is plain, written down for all to read. I am emotionally very subdued as I sit here writing these solemn words. My life is focused on being an encouragement to the many people I speak to and meet, but the dire warnings of Zephaniah must be restated. Too much of our "first world" behaviour mirrors the actions of the ancient world. The prophet's voice must be heeded. Our idolatrous, astrological, murderous and superstitious behaviour will not go unchecked forever.

Yet there is hope in this gloomy storm. God's mercy is available. *"Seek righteousness, seek humility; perhaps you will be sheltered on the day of the Lord's anger"* (2:1–3). God seeks our repentance. Herein lies our redemption.

The prophecy closes with a song about the grace, power and faithfulness of God. *"The LORD has taken away your punishment, he has turned back your enemies. The LORD ... is with you"* (3:15). What follows is one of the most fantastic statements of the Bible; huge and awesome, towering like a mountain amidst the words of Zephaniah's prophecy, *"The LORD your God is with you, He is mighty to save"* (3:17). His further comforting words amplify these truths.

> *"He will take great delight in you,*
>   *he will quiet you with his love,*
>   *he will rejoice over you with singing."*　　　　　　(3:17)

Then in a final crescendo:

> *"... I will deal*
>   *with all who oppressed you;*
> *I will rescue the lame*
>   *and gather those who have been scattered.*
> *I will give them praise and honour ...*
> *... I will gather you;*
>   *at that time I will bring you home ...*
> *... I* [will] *restore your fortunes*
>   *before your very eyes."*　　　　　　(3:19–20)

Many times I have seen these promises come true. I have watched with delight as people's damaged lives find forgiveness, restoration and wholeness. Their transformation is a fulfilment of these promises; fortunes restored, families renewed and hope regained. We have such a gracious, kind and forgiving God who, at the moment we turn to Him in sorrowful repentance, makes all His transforming power available to recreate our lives.

Zephaniah's prophecy had an impact on young King Josiah. *"In the eighth year of his reign,"* the Bible records, *"while he was still young, he began to seek the God of his father David"* (2 Chronicles 34:3). The young king of Zephaniah's day turned to the Lord with all his heart. Perhaps this in part is the reason for the triumphant, upbeat end to Zephaniah's prophecy. Later in his reign, Old Testament history records, *"Furthermore Josiah got rid of the mediums and spiritists, the household gods, the idols and all the other detestable things seen in Judah and Jerusalem"* (2 Kings 23:24–25). If the prophet Zephaniah has uncovered wrong actions and attitudes in our lives, may we have the humility to change our ways, to repent and turn to God who is mighty to save.

Questions to consider

▶ Do superstitions rule your life?

▶ Are you in danger of sacrificing precious things to Molech?

▶ Are there any idols in your life?

▶ Have you failed to enquire of the Lord?

▶ Are you held back by the words of a prediction?

Remember
The Lord your God is with you. He is mighty to save.

Notes

1. John Bright, *A History of Israel*, 3rd edn. (London: SCM Press Ltd, 1981), p. 312.
2. Melvin Rhodes, *America's Child Sacrifice*, at www.gnmagazine.org./issues/gn41/sacrifice.html
3. Allan Guttmacher Institute, *Sharing Responsibility: Women, Society and Abortion World Wide* (New York: AGI, 1999), p. 42.
4. Darrell Cosden, *Light and Salt – The Core Review*, Vol. 8, Issue 2, December 1996, p. 6.
5. Bill Hendrick, "Superstition can be hazardous to health, researchers find", at http://www.news-journalonline.com/2002/Mar/6/NOTE2.htm
6. Bill Hendrick, "Superstition can be hazardous to health, researchers find", at http://www.news-journalonline.com/2002/Mar/6/NOTE2.htm

Haggai
(520 BC)

❧ ❧

Chapter 10

First Things First

"Action expresses priorities"
(Mohandas Ghandi)

I am looking at the long-neglected foundations of a building. A project was started many years ago with enthusiasm, but was never finished. At the mercy of the elements, it lies dormant – an overgrown wilderness. A variety of emotions rise within me: frustration and disappointment at what could have been; sadness for wasted money and lost opportunity and embarrassment, for it was a Christian project and its failure brought shame and dishonour to God's work.

Haggai's dilemma, although similar, was much more serious. He stood in the capital city of Jerusalem, looking at the neglected foundations of the Temple of the Lord: the most spiritually significant building for the people of Israel. The Temple's neglect communicated contempt for God to the surrounding nations. "Peoples of the day measured how much another people thought of their god by how fine a temple they erected to him. As long as the temple remained destroyed and unattended, the testimony of the Jews was only negative."[1]

Almost two decades earlier things had been so different. After years in captivity subject to Babylonian oppression, the exiles were free to return home. Although the Israelites' faith was severely tested by their nation's downfall and subsequent exile, they had not lost hope. They had returned home with a new vision to restore their broken nation and rebuild the Temple of the Lord. There was excitement, energy and enthusiasm in the Israelite camp as they began to turn their vision into reality.

They began by building an altar, offering sacrifices to the Lord and laying the foundations for the Temple. But then it all stopped. Opposition, indifference, and dissatisfaction brought the project grinding to a halt. "However encouraging the first step may have been, the early years of the restoration venture proved bitterly disappointing, bringing frustration and discouragement. With even minimally modest expectations unfulfilled, as year followed disheartening year, the morale of the community sank dangerously."[2]

Enter Haggai. What a difference this plain-speaking man was to make. Haggai inspired the people to believe that the dream could be realised and that God's name could be honoured again.

The prophet began by bluntly speaking the truth to a pre-occupied and indifferent people: You have believed a lie (1:2), Your priorities are wrong (1:4), Your results are poor (1:6), *"You expected much, but see, it turned out to be little."* (1:9) You have been disobedient to God, but now it is time for you to *"give careful thought to your ways"* (1:5 and 7).

It was an honest review of the situation in direct and undisguised language. Haggai brought the people to a new understanding of how God regarded the neglected Temple and their preoccupation with their own affairs: *"'What you brought home, I blew away. Why?' declares the LORD Almighty. 'Because of my house, which remains a ruin, while each of you is busy with his own house'"* (1:9).

Wise people listen and respond positively to God's Word, even when drastic action is required. Haggai instructed the Israelites to go up into the mountains to bring down timber to build the Temple of the Lord. The people and their leaders obeyed (1:12). God's delight in the people's obedience was immediately expressed in His declaration, *"I am with you"* (1:13). He stirred up, invigorated and incited the people to work, giving them a new spirit and strength to build His Temple.

The restoration described in the book of Haggai reveals one of the great and consistent truths of the Bible: the passionate desire of God to live with us. Everyone came to realise that God wanted them to build His house. God's heart and passion have not changed. The New Testament challenges Christians: *"Do you not know that your body is a temple of the Holy Spirit, who is in you, whom you have received from God?"* (1 Corinthians 6:19); *"... you too are being built together to become a dwelling in which God lives by his Spirit"* (Ephesians 2:19–22). Haggai conveys God's passionate and timeless plea to all mankind: *"Rebuild the temple, that I may be pleased with it and glorified"* (1:8 NAS).

Haggai faced a second problem – discouragement. Some of the older people among the exiles had seen the splendour of Solomon's Temple when they were children, and were playing the dangerous game of making comparisons with yesteryear: "We'll never restore the Temple to what it was!" Haggai confronted them, *"Who of you is left who saw this house in its former glory? How does it look to you now? Does it not seem to you like nothing?"* (2:3). Looking to the future rather than the past, the prophet urges the exiles to be strong three times (2:4) and instructs them not to be afraid because God is with them (2:5). Having exhorted the exiles to keep going, Haggai reveals an encouraging and inspiring insight into the future to strengthen their determination to finish. He assured them that the Temple they were building would surpass the glory of Solomon's temple (2:9), and affirmed that wherever God is honoured and revered, true peace will abound (2:9).

Finally, through a series of questions, the prophet addressed the Israelites' dissatisfaction. He explained that evil, rather than holiness, is contagious (2:12–13). He told the people to take stock: to evaluate and measure their lives. Implicit in his questioning was the observation, "It has never been as good as you thought it was or wanted it to be" (2:16). He explained to the Israelites that an amazing transformation had taken place. *"Until now,"* he said, *"the vine and the fig-tree, the pomegranate and the olive tree have not borne fruit. 'From this day on I will bless you'"* (2:19). After a long period of expecting second best, economically, spiritually and relationally, everything changed!

It was a dramatic turn around resulting in the regeneration of a capital city and the rebirth of a nation. This all came about by a plain-speaking man bringing four prophetic messages, over a four-month period. One person made such a difference.

The following ten principles may be drawn from this ancient story and applied to our own lives.

1. God helps and blesses those who prioritise building His house

The New Testament boldly declares, *"Seek first his kingdom and his righteousness, and all these things will be given to you as well"* (Matthew 6:31–33). I have more than fifty years' worth of experience that testifies to this truth. My family and I, having tried our best to apply this principle throughout our lives, are utterly convinced that "all these things" have flowed to us as a direct result of prioritising our lives to seek first His kingdom – to live in obedience to His rule. Whether school fees, houses or spending money for holidays, God has always honoured His pledge to meet our needs; as long as we honoured Him by not being preoccupied by material things. God is no man's debtor.

2. Dramatic change can take place in desperate situations

It may have taken five years for the exiles to rebuild the Temple, but the transformation in their attitudes in response to Haggai's rebuke was almost instantaneous. History is full of incidences where the "odds" were dramatic. More often than not, it is brave and visionary people, like Haggai, who make all the difference. We must not allow desperate situations to darken our hope. This truth is confirmed by Malcolm Gladwell: "We need to prepare ourselves for the possibility that sometimes big changes follow from small events and that sometimes these changes can happen very quickly."[3]

3. Believing a lie has consequences

Jacob, the Old Testament patriarch, lived a depressed life for twenty years because he believed a lie concocted by his children that his own son, Joseph, was dead. His life became a self-inflicted misery because he believed one false report (Genesis 37:35). Individuals and nations have been held captive by lies.

Satan is the father of lies. He desires to poison us, to weaken us, to steal our joy and imprison us with his lies. God, however, is truth and truth brings freedom.

> "Doubt is a thief that makes us fear to tread
> where we might have won."
> *William Shakespeare*

4. Poor results in life may have a deeper, spiritual reason

The people of Haggai's day planted much but harvested little. They ate but were hungry, drank but were thirsty; the wages they earned disappeared, as if placed in purses full of holes. The return on their efforts was not as it should have been. Something was wrong.

Many people despair at the limited return they receive from their hard work. Unfortunately, in their quest to determine what went wrong, they rarely undertake a spiritual evaluation. As Christians, we must look beyond the presenting economic and relational issues, which are very real and must be addressed, to the deeper implications of how the priorities of our lives impact our use of time, money and talents.

5. Opposition and indifference can stop great projects

Every great idea will find opposition, just as any great leader will be attacked. Whether in the regeneration of a nation, the building of a great business, church or family, or the development of a new product or method, wise planners know that there will be opposition – people will almost always push back. The anti-slave trade movement, for example, suffered massive opposition from the rich slave-owners, traders and politicians. Yet – thank God – they did not crumble under the pressure of such great opposition.

Before we embark on our projects we must plan and find ways of staying inspired, focused and committed to crossing the finish line. We must not allow the weeds of life to overgrow what could be a magnificent building for God.

6. If you are thinking about starting a new project, be more committed to finishing it

There are two basic principles to completing and finishing tasks, plans and projects. The first is to start, the second is to keep going whatever happens.

John Bisagno has been pastoring First Baptist of Houston for a number of years. When John was just about to finish college, he was having dinner over at his fiancée's house one night. After supper, he was talking with his future father-in-law, Dr Paul Beck, out on the porch. Dr Paul Beck had been in ministry for years, and that was inevitably the subject toward which the conversation turned ... " It has been my experience [the older man said] that just one out of ten who start out in full-time service of the Lord at twenty-one are still on track by the age of sixty-five ... " The twenty year-old Bisagno was shocked. "I just can't believe that!" he said ... Bisagno told how he went home, took one the blank pages of his Scofield Reference Bible and wrote down the names of twenty-four young men who were his peers and contemporaries. These were young men in their twenties who were sold out for Jesus Christ ... Bisagno relates the following with a sigh: "I am now fifty-three years old. From time to time as the years have gone by, I've had to turn back to that page in my Bible and cross out a name. I wrote down those twenty-four names when I was just twenty years of age. Thirty-three years later, there are only three names remaining of the original twenty-four."[4]

7. Facing up to hard questions is sometimes painful, but has the possibility of amazing change

Through Haggai's ministry, the people of Judah reordered their priorities. Do not be afraid to face the difficult issues in your life. Tackle them and make a commitment to change. Surround yourself with friends and mentors who will support, comfort and assist you to deal with the hard questions in your life.

Nations also need to be brave beyond political preference to face the hard questions of societal breakdown and the poor results of past initiatives and strategies.

8. The implementation of a godly belief system carries God's promise of blessing

So many people live by their feelings, responding only to their emotions. These people are unpredictable, like a wave of the sea tossed by the wind (James 1:6). Others are more pragmatic, adopting the maxim, "If it isn't broke, don't fix it." They have no consistency of belief; they are driven by expediency and convenience. A godly belief system, featuring truth, integrity, honesty and self-control will provide a stable foundation, an ideal anchor, for both decision making and relationship building. The people of Haggai's day acted in obedience to God in accordance with a godly belief system and were blessed.

When a godly belief system is implemented it brings God's blessing. As a by-product, things work better to the pragmatists' approval, and things feel better to the emotionalists' satisfaction.

9. Understanding our "chosenness" has powerful possibilities

Since the beginning of time people have pondered the meaning of life. The same question has been asked time and time again: "Why am I here?" The Christian message brings real answers to life's big questions.

God has created you for a reason. He wants you to take hold of the purpose He has for your life.

The great "I am/I will" statements in the book of Haggai capture the heart of this wonderful message:

> "*I am with you*" (1:13; 2:4)
> "*I will fill this house with glory*" (2:7; 2:9)
> "*I will bless you*" (2:19)
> "*I will take you, I will make you*" (2:23).

God's final declaration *"for I have chosen you"* (2:23), is the rationale that summarises and explains each of the above statements.

God always operates with purpose. He begins because He already knows what will be accomplished.

Understand that God has chosen you. You may have ignored Him, avoided Him, or disobeyed Him, but none of this changes the fact that before you were born, God knew you, planned your life and provided everything you need to achieve the purpose for which you were born. Filled with this breath of life, let us rise up and confidently embrace life's powerful possibilities.

10. It is easier to become defiled than to stay holy

Through his dialogue in 2:11–13, Haggai illustrates the above principle which may be expressed more directly, "One rotten apple spoils the whole barrel". All the unspoilt apples cannot reverse the decay of the bad one.

The Western world has more than one rotten apple in its barrel. Decay is all around us, injuring and infecting millions. But how should we respond?

Henri Nouwen writes, "Our society is not a community radiant with the love of Christ but a dangerous network of domination and manipulation in which we can easily get entangled and lose our soul. The basic question is whether we ... have not already been so deeply moulded by the seductive powers of our dark world that we have become blind to our own and other people's fatal state and have lost the power and motivation to swim for our lives."[5] The apostle Paul put it this way, *"Don't let the world around you squeeze you into its own mould"* (Romans 12:2, Phillips translation).

We must recognise the challenges of living a holy life in a seductive and dark world. We must learn to identify and resist the pressures the world seeks to exert on us – the temptations to compromise a holy lifestyle – by fixing our eyes on God, allowing Him to transform us from the inside out. The benefits of this are a life rich in tranquillity, contentment and peace.

The prophet Haggai transformed the attitude of the people. This change unlocked the door to blessing and favour from God. But who will arrest our communities and usher in a "new day"? Who will catalyse our communities to function effectively? How long will we stare at the ruins of well-intentioned but unsuccessful initiatives to effect change? These forty-eight verses, penned over 2,500 years ago, offer some solutions to the problems of our society. The question remains: who will rise to the challenge?

Questions to consider

▶ Are your priorities in the right order?

▶ Are you building God's house in your life?

▶ Are the rewards for your work above or below expectations?

▶ Are you convinced that God has more blessing in your future?

▶ Have you believed any lies?

▶ Have you allowed opposition to thwart your dream?

Remember
If you build God's house, He will build your life.

Notes

1. Leon Wood, *The Prophets of Israel* (Schaumburg, IL: Regular Baptist Press, 1979).
2. John Bright, *A History of Israel* (London: SCM Press Ltd, 1980), p. 364.
3. Malcolm Gladwell, *The Tipping Point* (Abacus UK, 2001), p. 11.
4. Steve Farrar, *Finishing Strong* (Oregon: Multnomah Publishers, 1995), pp. 15–16.
5. Henri Nouwen, *The Way of the Heart* (HarperCollins, 1983).

Chapter 11

The Lord Comes

"To see clearly is poetry, prophecy and religion –
all in one"
(John Ruskin)

Two months had past since Haggai had delivered his prophecy. The city was a hive of activity. Construction had first begun on the temple when Zechariah arrived to deliver his message of repentance.

"This is what the LORD Almighty says: 'Return to me . . . and I will return to you'" (1:3). Zechariah urged the Israelites to turn from their evil practices – or face punishment – just as his predecessors had. The Israelites' reaction to the prophet's words was mixed, as their forefathers' had been.

Although Haggai's and Zechariah's prophecies have many parallels, there is a marked contrast in the styles of these prophets. Haggai was a pragmatist, a rough and ready builder responsible for the solid structure of the new Temple. His mission was to encourage the Jews to change their priorities and put God first. Zechariah, on the other hand, was more of an artist, adding colourful windows, stylish arches and bright and light interiors to the Temple. Zechariah calls for the moral rebuilding of a nation, beginning with an earnest national repentance. He reminds the citizens of the consequences of their forefathers' sins – captivity, pain and suffering.

The body of Zechariah's prophecy is much more expansive than that of Haggai's, and covers a much greater time frame. Zechariah's first eight chapters probably encompass a period of about three years, while the remaining chapters are considered to have been written up to forty years later.

The book of Zechariah is renowned for its messianic elements. There are more specific predictions relating to the promised Christ in Zechariah than in all the other minor prophets combined. Zechariah's book "... is the most messianic, the most truly apocalyptic and eschatological, of all the writings of the Old Testament."[2]

At a basic level, the book of Zechariah can be broken down into three sections: visions (chapters 1–6); instructional messages (chapters 7–8) and inspirational, messianic and apocalyptic prophecies and statements (chapters 9–14). Before examining these aspects of Zechariah's prophecy in further detail, allow me to offer you a brief flavour of his book.

October/November 520 BC: A call to repentance (1:1–6)

The names of the three generations of men mentioned in the opening verse of Zechariah's prophecy are of particular interest. People's names in Zechariah's day conveyed much more meaning and significance than Western society gives them today. Zechariah means, "The Lord Remembers"; his father, Berekiah means, "The Lord Blesses", and Iddo, his grandfather's name, means, "The Appointed Time". The prophet Zechariah was attempting to encourage the postexilic Judeans (and, indirectly, Christians today) by reassuring them that Jehovah, the covenant-keeping God, remembers and blesses those who remain faithful to him at His appointed time. What a positive thought with which to open a prophecy!

15th February 519 BC: Eight night visions (1:7–6:8)

The prophecy unfolds with Zechariah describing eight visions he received in one night. The overall momentum and intention of them was to inspire and encourage the people to complete the work of rebuilding the Temple. However, we would be unwise to conclude that these visions had relevance only to Zechariah's era.

At first the language of Zechariah can appear distant and difficult to comprehend, but we must persevere. Zechariah was a unique man, with both poetic and visionary gifts. God therefore spoke to him in a way that was appropriate for him, so that *he* could understand what God was communicating to him (albeit with the assistance of an angel). Each vision reveals an aspect of God's pervasive power to overcome the problems Zechariah's audience faced, instilling hope in those who were willing to listen. The following table outlines the essential elements of each of Zechariah's visions.

Ref.	Vision	Significance/Meaning
1:7–17	The man among the myrtle trees	God's special care for Israel; His plan to return to Jerusalem with mercy and to restore the city (and nation)
1:18–21	Four horns and four craftsmen	Israel's triumph over her enemies; the end of opposition to the re-building of the Temple
2:1–10	A man with a measuring line	Israel's future restoration will outgrow her city walls
3:1–10	Clean garments for the high priest	The high priest and the people of the land's sin will be forgiven
4:1–14	The gold lampstand and the two olive trees	The Lord will empower Israel by His Spirit
5:1–4	The flying scroll	Judgement for dishonesty and disobedience
5:5–11	The woman in a basket	God will carry away or remove Israel's sin and increase it upon or move it to Babylon
6:1–8	Four chariots	Judgement on the whole earth; God's protection for the faithful

Let's unpack a couple of these visions. Zechariah's second, that of the craftsmen coming to terrify the horns, opens to his audience the door of the unseen world – the often hidden rewards of obedience to God. As the craftsmen stand in opposition to ungodliness while building the Temple of the Lord, they terrify and overcome the opposing forces. As Christians we must see this verse as an encouragement for us to "terrify the horns"; to strive to lift the spiritual darkness from the people of our land.

The vision of a man with a measuring line must have given a tremendous boost to the postexilic generation. The city of Jerusalem was to be restored beyond the furthest reaches of their expectations (2:4). God is able to give us immeasurably more than we ask or imagine (Ephesians 3:20).

16th February 519 BC: Joshua, the high priest crowned (6:9–15)

Zechariah's third message was not a vision, but an historical act. It came as a summarising comment to the prophet's night visions. Zechariah was instructed to take the silver and gold that some of the returning exiles had brought from Babylon, and to make a crown for Joshua the high priest. God instructed Zechariah to place the crown on Joshua's head (6:12–13). Never before in Israel's history had the high priest been crowned king; thus, what Zechariah describes was a truly symbolic act with a significant messianic message.

Joshua was a representation of the coming Messiah. The "branch" inferred that the Messiah would sprout up from a humble place of birth, and that the messianic King–Priest's kingdom would be widespread. "He will ... build the temple of the LORD," refers almost exclusively to the Messiah because God had commissioned Zerubbabel, not Joshua, to rebuild the Temple. One fulfilment of this prophecy is identified by the apostle Paul in the New Testament, when he identifies Jesus Christ, the Messiah, as the chief cornerstone: *"In him the whole building is joined together and rises to become a holy temple in the*

Lord. And in him you too are being built together to become a
dwelling in which God lives by his Spirit" (Ephesians 2:19–22).

7th December 518 BC: A nation of hypocrisy to a nation of blessing (chapters 7–8)

Almost two years after his last message, Zechariah was
instructed by God to ask the people and the priests, *"Was it
really for me that you fasted?"* (7:5). Once again, the Israelites
were practising religious hypocrisy. Whether fasting or feasting,
their motives and intentions were wrong. Zechariah urged them
to change.

> *"This is what the LORD Almighty says: 'Administer true justice;*
> *show mercy and compassion to one another. Do not oppress the*
> *widow or the fatherless, the alien or the poor. In your hearts do*
> *not think evil of each other.' "*   (7:9–10)

Zechariah reminded the people of his generation of the
response of their forefathers, who stubbornly refused to listen
(7:11) and the punishment which their disobedience brought
them (7:14). God only desires genuine and sincere commitment,
not outward observance, or cold and callous hearts. He is not
impressed with our religious ways.

The second part of Zechariah's message is a much more
pleasant revelation. It characterises God's response to those
who hear and heed His message. Comforting words of encouragement, blessing and reconciliation with God: *"I will return to
Zion and dwell in Jerusalem"* (8:3). Zechariah portrays a wonderful
picture of a blessed people living in a blessed land, where old
people are content and the streets are full of children playing in
safety (8:4–5). A community based on godly values was to be
built (8:16–17).

When the worship of God is at the heart and centre of
people's lives, and they love truth and peace, righteousness and
integrity, everything is blessed, and all can live in peace and
tranquillity.

c. 480 BC: Advent, rejection and reception of the Messiah, Jesus Christ (chapters 9–14)

The remaining six chapters can be divided into two distinct prophecies: the coming of the Messiah and His rejection (chapters 9–11); and the coming of the Messiah, His reception and rule (chapters 12–14). These chapters "deal with the same subject matter ... the overthrow of world powers and the final supremacy of the nation of Israel. The first part is more general in its presentation and stresses the overthrow of the powers; the second is more specific and stresses Israel's final purification and supremacy."[3]

Chapters 9–11 foretell that God, the Priest–King will visit His people in mercy, and the nations in judgement. Zephaniah prophesised the coming of the Messiah to shepherd His flock, only to be rejected (Zephaniah 2:6). As a result of this rebellion Zechariah explained, the people of God would experience great suffering.

Chapters 12–14 prophetically describe the victories in the coming Day of the Lord. There are three apocalyptic pictures:

1. Jerusalem will be saved from a siege at the hands of her enemies by the intervention of God.

2. A remnant of Israel will be saved.

3. The nations will come to Jerusalem to share in the joyous feast of tabernacles and all will enjoy the blessing of God.

Messianic statements

There are an astounding number of messianic statements in Zechariah's prophecy. We are very privileged to be able to examine many of them with the benefit of hindsight. They would have been an incredible reassurance and encouragement of God's plan for salvation and justice for the people of Zechariah's day. For us, as well as retaining this function, they also serve as a powerful indication and proof of the divine authorship of the Scriptures and therefore as a testimony to the trustworthiness of their message. As the examples in the box illustrate, anyone can make a prediction. It is when these predictions are fulfilled that we should pay most attention.

Famous false predictions[4]

"Unworthy of the attention of practical and scientific men."
*British Parliamentary Committee report on
Thomas Edison's electric light bulb*

"X-rays will prove to be a hoax."
Lord Kelvin, President of the Royal Society, 1883

"The 'telephone' has too many shortcomings to be seriously considered as a means of communication.
The device is inherently of no value to us."
Western Union internal memo, 1876

Biblical scholars have determined that Jesus fulfilled every one of the estimated four hundred and fifty six identifying characteristics of the Messiah.

The Professor Emeritus of Science at Westmont College, Peter Stoner, has calculated that the probability of Jesus fulfilling only eight of the messianic prophecies is 1 in 10^{17} (a one followed by 17 zeros). To get a feel for this figure, Professor Stoner provides the picture of the entire state of Texas being filled with silver dollars to a depth of two feet, marking one of them, mixing them all up and asking a blindfolded person to select, on his first attempt, the marked coin.[5]

One of the most precise fulfilments of messianic prophecy is characterised when we celebrate Palm Sunday in the Christian calendar: the triumphal entry of the Messiah. On this day, some 500 years after Zechariah's prophecy, Jesus Christ rode into Jerusalem on a colt, the foal of a donkey (Matthew 21:1–11), just as Zechariah predicted (9:9).

In the following chapter, Zechariah prophesied that "From Judah will come the cornerstone" (10:4). Zechariah painted a unique picture of the Messiah as a "cornerstone and capstone" – an image reiterated by the New Testament writers (Ephesians 2:20; 1 Peter 2:4–8; Matthew 21:42). The New Testament proclaims Jesus as the cornerstone that regulates the dimensions of the building and the grand capstone that finishes it.

What is the price of betrayal? Zechariah prophesied *"thirty pieces of silver"* (11:12). He predicted Judas' dreadful betrayal with startling accuracy (Matthew 26:14–16). His prophecy of the betrayal continues, *"And the LORD said to me, 'Throw it to the potter'"* (11:13). The selling of Jesus for the stated price and the fate of this awful "blood money" confirm the accuracy of Zechariah's prediction: *"So Judas threw the money into the temple and left ..."* (Matthew 27:5) and the chief priests, as Zechariah indicated, purchased a potter's field with the money (Matthew 27:7).

After Jesus' betrayal and trial, came His sacrificial death. Hanging on the cross, nails in His hands and feet, He breathed His final breath. To make sure He was dead, one of the soldiers pierced His side bringing a sudden flow of blood and water (John 19:34). Zechariah points to this substitutionary sacrifice in three settings. Firstly, he prophesised, *"They will look on me the one they have pierced"* (12:10; see John 19:36–37). *"On that day a fountain will be opened to the house of David and the inhabitants of Jerusalem, to cleanse them from sin and impurity"* (13:1). And finally, in relation to this sacrifice he says, *"If someone asks him, 'What are these wounds on your body?' he will answer, 'The wounds I was given at the house of my friends'"* (13:6).

The final chapter of Zechariah's prophecy promises that a day is coming when the Lord will go out to fight against the nations gathered in Jerusalem (14:3). On that day, Zechariah prophesised, when the Lord *"will stand on the Mount of Olives"* (14:4) massive geological events will follow: rocks will split apart and living water will flow. On this day, *"The LORD will be king over the whole earth ... there will be one LORD, and his name the only name"* (14:9). Having clearly identified Jesus in the earlier messianic statements it is reasonable to conclude that the "as yet unfulfilled" parts of Zechariah's prophecy also apply to Him and will be fulfilled.

Apocalyptic statements

The book of Zechariah is rich in apocalyptic statements. In order to be concise, I will highlight only two of them:

1. *" 'In the whole land,' declares the* Lord, *'two thirds will be struck down and perish; yet one third will be left in it' "* (13:8).

    Until the dawn of the atomic age and the development of chemical and biological warfare, many people thought that this prediction was far-fetched. Whether it will be fulfilled by these means or not, the creation of these "weapons of mass destruction" has certainly brought a fresh understanding of the possible fulfilment of this prophecy as we enter the twenty-first century.

2. *"This is the plague with which the* Lord *will strike the nations that fought against Jerusalem: Their flesh will rot while they are still standing on their feet, their eyes will rot in their sockets, and their tongues will rot in their mouths"* (14:12).

    The atomic bombs dropped on Japan in 1945 had more or less exactly the effects described above on a vast number of people. Again, I am not concluding that these apocalyptic prophecies mean that nuclear explosions will take place – they may or may not. I am merely asserting that these apparently impossible circumstances prophesied to the ancient world are distinctly possible in the world of today.

Regardless of your interpretation of the meaning of these apocalyptic statements, do not lose the urgency of their message. The Lord Jesus came once. He is coming again, and His return will be glorious and terrifying.

As Zechariah's poetic prophecy draws to a close, he uses his final words to assure the people that the Lord was coming. Coming to be with them, to fill the temple with the glory of His presence. Jesus came in glory to them, when He came in humility in

Bethlehem. Jesus, the Son of God, will come again in great glory. In response to this assurance, I humbly offer this advice alongside great saints from the past: live every day as though He were coming today and plan every day as if He were not coming for a long time. This balance, I believe, will assist us to keep the priorities of our lives in line with the will and purpose of God. The New Testament believers often shared a greeting, "Marantha" – "Come, O Lord!" (1 Corinthians 16:22; Revelation 22:20) – perhaps we should too!

Questions to consider

▶ Is the Lord's coming important to you?

▶ Are you filled with God's Spirit?

▶ Do you know the Messiah personally?

▶ Are you convinced of the relevance of prophecy?

Remember
God is not slack concerning His promise.
Jesus is coming again.

Notes

1. Chapters 9–14 of Zechariah's prophecy are considered to have been written on or after 480 BC due to Zechariah's mention of Greece (9:13) which only entered public awareness to any real significance after the battle of Salamis in 480 BC.
2. George Robinson, *The International Bible Encyclopaedia* (1949), ed., s.v. "Zechariah, Book of", in *Dr Constable's Notes on Zechariah*, 2002 Edition, p. 5 at http://www.soniclight.com/constable/notes/pdf/zechariah.pdf
3. Leon J. Wood, *The Prophets of Israel* (Baker Book House Co., 1987), p. 372.
4. From www.ozsermonillustrations.com/illustrations/ famous_false_predictions.htm
5. *Science Speaks "Scientific Proof of the Accuracy of Prophecy and the Bible"* by Peter W. Stoner, MS, and Robert C. Newman, STM, Ph.D. (Chicago: Moody Press, 1976).

MALACHI
(c. 450–420 BC)

≈∂⊘ ⊘∂≈

Chapter 12

Carelessness Costs

*"Discouragement is not the absence of adequacy
but the absence of courage."*
(Neal A. Maxwell)

Malachi is the last of a noble line of courageous men who dared to make a difference; men who dared to speak out knowing the perilous repercussions they would face as a result of their brave obedience to God. Malachi's message was to echo in the four hundred years of prophetic silence that followed, until its further fulfilment in the person of John the Baptist.

Malachi had an awkward task. The carelessness of the priests and people toward God in his generation was an easy target to hit. Helping them understand and face the deeper issues of the nation's malaise required more thought and care. The enthusiasm of the Jewish people to rebuild the Temple and the nation, catalysed by Haggai and Zechariah, had dwindled. Discouragement had set in. The zeal these prophets engendered had ebbed away.

Haggai and Zechariah had spoken of a glorious future. They promised the Jewish people that God would come and establish His kingdom among them. The people had seen some of the prophecies fulfilled, but the full splendour of the promised, glorious future was not yet realised. The people had allowed the passing of time to crush their hope. Despondency, disappointment and dejection was widespread. They doubted

God's love (1:2). They no longer trusted His justice (2:17). Their confession was inaccurate (3:14–15).

The passage of time, and the Jews belief that God had let them down, provided fertile conditions for carelessness and indifference. Their worship degenerated into ritual observance, the practice of tradition rather than heartfelt obedience and reverence for God's Law. As one commentator writes, "The Jews ... were cured, by the captivity of their idolatry, but prone to neglect the House of God. The priests had become lax and degenerate, sacrifices were inferior, tithes were neglected, and the people had reverted to their old practice of intermarrying with their idolatrous neighbours ... Discouraged by their weakness, wedded to their sins, the Jews had settled down, in a lethargic state of mind, to await the coming of the Promised Messiah."[1] Loss of hope, discouragement and disappointment had led to very careless living. Covenants and agreements in marriage and business were broken. The Jewish people had become selfish law-breakers.

As the decades passed they felt less and less important. They lived in a small province in the backwaters of the still great Persian Empire. They had been told they were a special people but they felt inferior. They had been promised great blessing but they felt cursed. They had been encouraged to be people of covenant and commitment but carelessness seemed easier and more comfortable. It was into this situation of apathy, inferiority and despondency that Malachi spoke words of warning, condemnation and encouragement.

The people of Malachi's day were discouraged because the prophecies of yesteryear were not fulfilled in the way they expected. Discouragement is an enemy whatever provokes its manifestation. Sometimes our dreams and expectations don't reach the high water mark of our hopes. Sometimes people don't live up to our expectations and we become disillusioned. We would be wise to learn from Malachi's story, otherwise their discouragement will become ours and our confession will echo the lie, *"It is futile to serve God"* (3:14).

Each of us will encounter discouragement and disappointment

many times in our lives. However, when we meet these twin enemies we are not excused from living right with God, others and ourselves. What then should we use as an antidote and remedy in the many situations that conspire to render us discouraged? The simple answer is, "Take courage!" The Bible records that when King David was discouraged by an awful situation, he *"encouraged himself in the Lord"* (1 Samuel 30:6 AV). Likewise, we must take courage from knowing who God is and who we are. He loves us with an everlasting love and is committed to our personal development. Another key David teaches us, is to confess and rehearse our past victories, as he did before his battle with Goliath (1 Samuel 17:34–37). When discouragement says, "Stop, give up. It's not worth it," we need to be *"strong and very courageous"*, as the Lord exhorted Joshua (Joshua 1:7). This is the exercise of our will over the inclinations of our feelings. Otherwise, living in the land of discouragement will rob us of more than we realise and will open the door to other deadly symptoms of limitation.

We earlier established that if you ask the wrong question, you will get the wrong answer. Malachi further teaches us the importance of the wise use of questions. He uses them in his prophecy in a conversational style, confronting the Jews sarcastic mindset. The prophet makes bold statements; confessing God's love for the people (1:2), questioning them about their contempt for His name (1:6) and accusing them of robbery (3:8). The peoples' answers are how, what and when questions.

The technique of using a question to answer a question has been used successfully by many people, including Jesus. The prophet uses it to bring the people to a greater understanding of their poor relationship with God.

God has chosen to use questions in this and other ways throughout the Bible. In Genesis, God asks Adam and Eve as they attempt a cover up, *"Where are you?"* (Genesis 3:9). The question was not for God's benefit. He knew perfectly well where they were. The question was to help them to understand their position and the consequences of their actions. Jesus also used questions to powerful affect. In our family homes, our class-rooms of learning, our boardrooms of decision-making, or in our making disciples we need right answers. We must therefore use the power of questions well.

A third lesson we can learn from Malachi is the importance of honouring God. It is God who gave us life, saved us in Jesus Christ and sustains our existence. The infectious "take it for granted" attitude of many around us, and the busyness of our lives, must not be allowed to distract our attention from worshipping and honouring God. *"How have we shown contempt for your name?"* (1:6) and *"How have we defiled you?"* (1:7) the priests ask. God answers, "By bringing inadequate offerings . . . Instead of giving the best you gave the worst, the lame, blind, crippled and diseased animals for sacrifice" (1:8). So many people exercise ignorance of the fact that *"Every good and perfect gift is from above"* (James 1:17) and that the power and ability to make wealth is a gift from God (Deuteronomy 8:17–18).

> "God gave me my money.
> I believe the power to make money is a gift from God."
> *John D. Rockefeller*

Sadly, some of us are so selfish that we make no offering to honour God or sacrifice to help the less privileged. Many give God and others only the small change of life; whatever is left over. In these practices we dishonour God. Malachi insists that we have cursed ourselves: *"'Cursed is the cheat who has an acceptable male in his flock and vows to give it, but then sacrifices a blemished animal to the Lord. For I am a great king,' says the Lord Almighty, 'My name is to be feared among the nations'"* (1:14).

Can a Christian rob God? Yes, as the dialogue recorded in the book of Malachi reveals: *"In tithes and offerings. You are under a*

curse – the whole nation of you – because you are robbing me" (3:8).
The Jewish people had failed to maintain the practice of tithing,
giving God ten per cent of their income, and they were cursed as
a result.

Many Christians understand some of the principles of giving.
When challenged about tithing some misguidedly say, "But I am
not living under law, I am living under grace." There are two
immediate responses to such a statement. The first is that tithing
preceded the law (Genesis 14:20) and the second is to understand the New Testament truth that grace is more than law
(Hebrews 7:2–6). Those who are living "under grace" should do
more than tithe.

In fifty years as a Christian I have lost count of the number of
people I have witnessed reap a plentiful harvest as a result of
giving to God's work. They share amazing stories of miraculous
provision and repaid debts. Although mathematically ridiculous, those who practise living on less than ninety per cent
testify that they are better off than when they lived on one
hundred per cent. This reflects the truth expressed by God
through Malachi in a biblically unique challenge: *"'Test me in
this,' says the* Lord *Almighty, 'and see if I will not throw open the
floodgates of heaven and pour out so much blessing that you will not
have room for it'"* (3:10–11). I have come to understand that by
robbing God, we rob God of an opportunity to bless us.

Our seaplane touched down on the Amazon river in Brazil. We
enjoyed a morning service in the village church and were invited
into the minister's very humble home, the venue for our after-
noon lunch and fellowship. During our first moments of greeting the minister's family at the entrance to their home, another
villager came to the door. After a short conversation with the
minister, he handed over some money and went on his way.
"That's the village baker," the minister said. "He comes and pays
his tithes every week." The minister explained to me that this
man was not a member of the Church, or even a Christian, but
he firmly believed and had proved to himself that it is wise to

obey God by bringing tithes to His work. Start bringing ten per cent of your income and wealth to God and see what happens. You will be very surprised.

The community of the saints, the body of Christ, is an amazing entity. In every continent on this planet I have been welcomed into both humble and palatial homes, often by people I had never previously met. On almost every occasion I have been treated as a member of their family. Christian fellowship is wonderful – there is nothing quite like it on earth. In his concluding remarks, Malachi writes, *"Then those who feared the Lord talked with each other, and the Lord listened and heard"* (3:16). His words suggest that God is stimulated to action by the holy meeting together of His people: *"They will be mine . . . I will spare them"* (3:17).

In a world full of lonely people, we need to value Christian fellowship, whatever form it takes, whether the power of corporate worship, the intimacy of sharing bread and wine, the power of unity in intercession, the celebration of the "rites of passage" with joy and thankfulness; and, of course, the delight of simply being together, laughing with those who laugh and crying with those who cry. The Bible lays down a valuable exhortation for us:

> *"Let us not give up meeting together, as some are in the habit of doing, but let us encourage one another – and all the more as you see the Day approaching."*   (Hebrews 10:25)

Picture the scene, people leaping and rejoicing like *"calves released from the stall"* (4:2). Malachi's picture is one of freedom, fulfilment and victory. He has gazed into the future and seen a time when righteousness is established. A time when the proud and arrogant receive justice. A time when wrongs are righted. The picture which Malachi gives us has several justifiable interpretations.

Firstly, it can be seen as a parable of salvation: the transformation in a person when they accept the Lordship of Jesus; the debt and penalty of personal sin removed.

Secondly, we can view it as a picture of God's ability to transform impossible situations; to break the chains of restriction and the barriers of limitation. The Christian gospel is the only religion that claims "signs and wonders" (the miraculous) as a component of its message. Whether for individuals trapped in addictions, or nations under the heel of an enemy or in the grip of plague, God's power can transform the situation.

Finally, it speaks of a day that is coming when every man, woman and child will be asked to account for the sins they have committed before the King of Glory. Every sin must be paid for. Righteousness and justice will prevail. All who revered His name and knew Him as Lord, the martyred or murdered, unseen and unknown, famous or forgotten, will leap like calves released from a stall, as the Kingdom of God comes in all its glory.

God hates divorce (2:16). He made the Jewish people aware of His displeasure at the sight of marriages breaking down:

> *"He* [the Lord] *no longer pays attention to your offerings ... You ask, 'Why?' It is because the* LORD *is acting as the witness between you and the wife of your youth, because you have broken faith with her, though she is your partner, the wife of your marriage covenant."*   (2:13–14)

Words fail to describe the pain God feels at the millions of unnecessary divorces that take place in the civilised world every year. Western society has millions of children who have been fathered but are now fatherless.

> In 1999 there were 145,000 divorces (400 per day) granted in England and Wales. Of these divorcing couples, 55% had at least one child.[2]

> The National Fatherhood Initiative reports that, in America, 43%
> of first marriages dissolve within fifteen years; about 60% of
> divorcing couples have children; and approximately one million
> children each year experience the divorce of their parents.[3]
>
> Twenty-four million [American] children [34%] live in homes
> without their biological fathers. That means that tonight, one out
> of every three children will go to bed in a home in which their
> father does not live.[4]
>
> It is estimated that 40% of these children, children in father-
> absent homes, have not seen their father at all in the past year.[5]

It is therefore wonderfully encouraging to know that a power
exists to change these awful situations. This power is identified
in the closing words of Malachi's prophecy: *"He will turn the
hearts of the fathers to their children, and the hearts of the children to
their fathers."* But for those who reject this re-uniting grace, a
chilling warning is issued: *"or else I will come and strike the land
with a curse"* (4:6). The catalyst for this breakthrough is the
"arrival" of the prophet Elijah, a challenging concept to grasp.
Permit me to explain.

The New Testament recognises John the Baptist as the forerunner of the fulfilment of Malachi's words (Luke 1:17; Matthew
11:13–14; 17:12–13).

Elijah brought a message of repentance accompanied by many
signs and wonders. John the Baptist, in preparing for Jesus' public
arrival spoke a direct message calling all people to repentance.
The "Elijah Spirit" continues to speak in our day, through God's
prophets, calling fathers back to their children and preparing the
way for the return of Jesus Christ.

The social consequences of the appalling and alarming rate of
breakdown in families is difficult to quantify. The emotional
pain, largely unseen, causes perhaps the greatest damage.
Malachi says that if we continue along the road of more and
more broken families, our land will be struck with a curse. The
breakdown of the family will continue to reap a rotten harvest,
exacting a high price from all parties involved: parents, children

and the society in which they live. "The broken home ranks higher than any other problem in explaining why pupils are struggling at school. If this is what it is like now, what is it going to be like in 10 to 20 years time?"[6]

The American criminologist Robert Sampson has been able to show that a city's divorce rate is actually a better predictor of the robbery rate than statistics of arrest and sentencing.[7]

Dr Patrick Dixon has calculated an estimate of the total economic cost of the breakdown of the family to Britain. He reached a total of £9 billion in 1995. Working on the basis that trends would slow down by 50% (which seems very unlikely given present trends), he predicts costs of a further £110 billion from 1996–2005.[8]

Official statistics simply highlight how the institution of marriage has broken down. In Britain, for the first time since records began, the number of households headed by a married couple has fallen below 50%. In recent decades the decline in the number of married couples has been acute. As we entered the new millennium, just over half of the British population was married – compared to more than two thirds in 1970. The cause of the breakdown is twofold – an increase in divorce and more couples choosing to live together than marry.[9]

Although our society may reject marriage, God remains committed to it. It is His idea. He is a God of covenant – honouring the promises He makes to us and we make to each other. God is willing to bless any marriage – whether Christian or non-Christian. A society returning to family values, upholding the sanctity of marriage, will reap a reward.

Without attending to the spiritual demands and prophetic obligations that God has made clear to us, no amount of money, resources or ingenuity will solve our social problems.

Question to consider

► Has disappointment stopped your progress?

► Has God asked a question you have not answered?

► Is the principle of honour important to you?

► Are you committed to your promises?

► Are you enjoying the blessing of being a giver?

► Are you taking care or taking courage?

Remember
God loves a cheerful giver.

Notes

1. Halley's Bible Handbook (Grand Rapids: Zondervan, 1961).
2. "Changing Trends in Family Life", CARE Factsheet, p. 3, at www.care.org.uk/resource/docs/res_familytrends.htm
3. National Fatherhood Initiative: Father Facts, 4th ed. Top Ten Father Facts www.fatherhood.org/fatherfacts/topten.htm
4. National Fatherhood Initiative: Father Facts, 4th ed., Introduction at www.fatherhood.org/fatherfacts/intro.htm
5. National Fatherhood Initiative: Father Facts, 4th ed. Top Ten Father Facts www.fatherhood.org/fatherfacts/topten.htm
6. *The Times*, 6th October, 1998, in "For Better or for Worse: A look at marriage, cohabitation and family breakdown", CARE Conference Paper at www.care.org.uk/resource/docs/paper_marriage.htm
7. R. Sampson, "Does an Intact Family Reduce Burglary Risks for its Neighbours", *Sociology and Social Research*, Vol. 71, 1987, pp. 404–407, reported in Whelan and de Burgh, "The Necessary Family and How to Support it", *Family and Youth Concern*, 1996, p. 29 in "For Better or for Worse: A look at marriage, cohabitation and family breakdown", CARE Conference Paper at www.care.org.uk/resource/docs/paper_marriage.htm
8. Dixon, *The Rising Price of Love: The True Cost of the Sexual Revolution* (Hodder and Stoughton, 1995), p. 191 in "For Better or for Worse: A look at marriage, cohabitation and family breakdown", CARE Conference Paper at www.care.org.uk/resource/docs/paper_marriage.htm
9. *Census 2001*, National Office of Statistics.

Conclusion

The voices of these brave men have fallen silent. Their pens have stopped writing. It would be 400 years before one of God's prophets was to be so powerfully heard again. My work in expressing a contemporary interpretation of their words is also finished.

What have we learned, and what will we do? They are dead, yet they still speak. They were wise; will we listen? Having looked back, will we take heed? As we look forward, will we change? The sun will rise on a better tomorrow if we do.

The prophets called for obedience to God's Word and repentance for past failure. They called for answers to hard questions. It must be the same today, for if we do not take responsibility by definition we are irresponsible. Be sure of this, Western civilisation as it stands will not continue, forgetting and ignoring God, without consequences. Judgement is coming. It is time to obey.

If we respond in obedience, we will see the other face of God, smiling with mercy and kindness. He will heal our broken society using the same power that created all things in the beginning. If we ignore God's Word, the implications will have long-term consequences and could be very painful. What decisions are you making now that will positively or negatively influence future generations of your family and community?

Indifference and a laissez-faire approach to God's demands will bear negative fruit in the future. God "hates" seedless grapes! Part of the supernatural outworking of creation is that God has placed the future inside the present. What will your future be?

If you have enjoyed this book and would like to help us to send a copy of it and many other titles to needy pastors in the **Third World**, please write for further information or send your gift to:

**Sovereign World Trust
PO Box 777, Tonbridge
Kent TN11 0ZS
United Kingdom**

or to the **'Sovereign World'** distributor in your country.

Visit our website at **www.sovereign-world.org**
for a full range of Sovereign World books.